WHY CAN'T I TELL YOU WHO I REALLY AM?

WHY CAN'T I TELL I YOU WHO I REALLY AM?

ROBERT R. BALL

WORD BOOKS
PUBLISHER
WACO, TEXAS

A DIVISION OF
WORD, INCORPORATED

First Printing—July 1977
Second Printing—September 1977
Third Printing—November 1977
First Paperback Printing—August 1978
Second Paperback Printing—October 1984

WHY CAN'T I TELL YOU WHO I REALLY AM?
Formerly published under the title, *The "I Feel" Formula,*

Library of Congress Catalog Card Number: 77-07453

ISBN 0-8499-3001-4

Printed in the United States of America

Dedicated with pleasure and appreciation to
Bobby, Dianne, Randy, and Nancy,
once my children—now
"I feel"
my perceptive teachers, loving supporters,
and treasured friends

ACKNOWLEDGMENTS

Sometimes it happens that biblical study and practical need intersect in a helpful, amazing, *providential* way. It was such a moment which provided the insight around which this book was built.

For his wise, patient, and helpful guidance in developing the biblical basis, I am deeply indebted to Dr. Herman Waetjen of San Francisco Theological Seminary, and to Roy Fairchild, also of SFTS, who had earlier gotten me started in an appreciation of the mutual edification existing between theology and psychology.

A number of close friends—more than I can now remember—in the Memorial Drive Presbyterian Church in Houston, Texas, read and commented on the manuscript at various stages of its preparation. This, along with the love and encouragement of that whole, magnificent congregation of God's people, was of indispensable value. Though I was their pastor, they allowed me to be human and helped me straddle the human and divine aspects of the gospel.

Two beautiful and buoyant ladies, first Edith Little and then Gloria Russell, spent long, but at least from my standpoint not thankless, hours typing and retyping these pages. For all this coaching, caring, and cooperation, I want to acknowledge my appreciation, unmistakably personal and immeasurably profound.

CONTENTS

WHY CAN'T I TELL YOU WHO I REALLY AM?

1

"GOD ALMIGHTY" STATEMENTS

"Please understand how much I hurt! If only you could know that behind my sometimes angry, sometimes kind façade I'm longing for your respect and approval. You think I'm rational and calm? You say I've got it all together? If only you knew! Torment and confusion swirl around in the depths of me. I want so much to be understood and accepted. I'd give almost anything!"

Would you guess who said that? A president of the United States, a famous movie queen, a superstar athlete? Or was it a learned philosopher, a mixed-up teenager, or a man of great wealth? You're right, whomever you guessed. It was all of these, but you're the one in whom I'm most interested. Didn't I hear you say those things just the other day? Or was it night? You didn't think anyone was around to hear you? And besides, you didn't say it out loud.

No, I'm not a psychic, and I can't read your mind. But if you didn't say the above statements, or something very close, you're one of the most remarkable and unusual persons in the whole world—or else you do a fantastically successful job of kidding yourself as well as everyone else.

About a dozen years ago I was in the midst of great inner turmoil. Right at the moment I can't recall just what the situation was that occasioned my distress. I do remember, vividly, that about two in the morning I was up prowling around through my dark and sleeping household, and I said, to no one but the impersonal darkness, "I think I'm going out of my mind. I must be the most insecure person in the whole world."

Later that day I attended a luncheon for clergymen and physicians. The speaker was a man who had spent his entire professional career as a hospital chaplain. He had pioneered in that field and was now a widely respected author and lecturer. In the midst of describing the usual steps a person goes through during a depression, the man said, "When a person reaches the bottom, he or she will frequently say things like, 'I think I'm going out of my mind. I must be the most insecure person in the whole world.' It's very normal."

That man, for all his brilliance and experience, is not a psychic. Nor had he bugged my house. He had never met or heard of me. He was simply a sensitive person who had spent a lot of time getting in touch with the depths of people's lives—and with his own depths. The experience that was profoundly unique and personal to me is common to all humankind. Without ever having met me, this man understood me better than most people who knew me well.

One of the most influential psychologists in America, Carl Rogers, looking back over what he had learned during a long professional career, concluded, "That which is most personal is also most general." [1] When you and I get

---

1. Carl Rogers, *On Becoming a Person* (Boston: Houghton Mifflin Co., 1961), p. 26.

in touch with the deepest and most personal meaning in our lives, that's when we're most likely to perceive what's really going on in the depths of others.

All my experiences as a pastor confirm this insight. When people walk out after a Sunday morning sermon and say "You were really talking to me this morning" or "My wife must have told you about the conversation we had last night," I know I have been addressing the gospel to the problems going on in me. "That which is most personal is also most general."

When I say I'm certain you have a deep longing to be understood, that's my basis. I've recognized that hunger in myself, and I've experienced it in every other person I've been permitted to know well.

Not being understood is painful. It makes lonely people of many who are surrounded by bushels of friends and acres of activities. But what happens when we do crank up our courage and reach out for understanding and friendship? Often we're told to take up an interesting hobby or read a good book. Then we're hesitant to reach out again.

We can also experience the loneliness of not being understood in the midst of a great happiness. Something has happened that fills us with joy, hope, and confidence. We want to share it; but, more frequently than you might suppose, the ones with whom we want to share look at us as if we're a little off our rocker—like we don't really understand the problem or we wouldn't be so joyful.

But there are times, and I hope you've known some of them, when we do experience being understood, deeply and personally. Even when I was at the bottom of my depression, and even though I had never before seen the speaker, the fact that another human being did understand what I was going through ripped me out of my isolation. When understanding comes in a personal way, face-to-face, you find yourself feeling that life has few things to offer more wonderful than that. What a joy it is to feel understood and accepted!

That's what this book is about—discovering why we are so seldom understood and developing our capacities for being understood and understanding. It has to do with growth as a whole human being, a process that is never over but during which we experience many exciting and satisfying gains. In other words, this is a book about communication—about communion and about how we come together with other persons and with ourselves.

Most people from whom we seek understanding are so busy trying to be understood themselves that they have little inclination or time to spend understanding us. There's not much we can do about that. We can say, "Won't you please listen to me?" We can get angry. It's not likely, though, that either of these will help very much.

However, there's another thing we can do something about: One of the biggest reasons people fail to understand us is that *we seldom say what we mean!* We may think we do, but chances are we don't.

We may be loud and emphatic. We may talk all the time. But seldom do any of us say what we mean. Often we don't even know what we mean!

Think of the last time you got angry with your spouse. What did you say? Was it something like "That was the stupidest trick I have ever seen in my life"? That's emphatic, all right, but is it what you meant? Was it in fact, of all the experiences you have had in your life, the one most lacking in rational judgment? Probably not. Well, what did you mean? We'll get into that later. For now, would you be willing to entertain the idea, just as a possibility, that one reason people fail to understand us is that we seldom say what we really mean?

One afternoon I was having lunch with a psychologist friend. In the course of our conversation he said, "I've about decided that the only thing words are good for is lying." I'm sure he didn't mean it literally, but I'm also sure he was serious. When you put together all the words you hear in a single day (even if you are not a professional counselor who is paid to listen), what have you got? Usually a lot of rationalizations, excuses, and defensive justifications. People are saying something, but what they are saying is seldom what they mean.

The title of this chapter, "'God Almighty' Statements," is the term I employ to characterize most human conversation. We make "God Almighty" statements instead of saying what we mean. If you could sit back for a moment as a detached observer and listen to the conversations in your family, most of them, I'll bet, would come out something like this:

"Nobody understands me!"

"You never get home on time!"

"Junior is absolutely impossible!"

"You don't care one thing about me or the kids!"

"Other wives don't treat their husbands that way!"

"Your mother won't leave me alone!"

"I just wish you'd pick up your clothes once in a while!"

"The church isn't interested in anything but money!"

"You never listen to me!"

"Things just aren't like they used to be!"

"You are the biggest nagger in town!"

"If he (or she!) gets elected, this country is finished!"

"Nobody cares about doing good work any more!"

I call these "God Almighty" statements. It's like the heavens open, and these words drop down from on high as if spoken by God himself. Every one of them purports to be incontrovertible fact. They leave no room for exception or reservation. They give the impression "That's the way it is!"

And we wonder why we can't get any vital communication going in our families! How can you respond to a "God Almighty" statement? If you have a "God Almighty" statement thrown at you, you have only three choices: you can duck and run, in the hope that it will never hit you; you can submit and accept it ("You're right. I'm just no good."); or you can stand up and fight back with a "God Almighty" statement of your own. I don't know which of these three options occurs most frequently, but they are equally frustrating and nonproductive.

A "God Almighty" statement is never authentic. Who can speak with the wisdom and authority of God? (This includes preachers although they are usually among the worst offenders!) No matter how long I have spent studying you, no matter how great my analytical skills, I will never be able to say with absolute authority, "That's the way you are!" I can have hunches, seasoned with insight and experience, but when I begin to think I've got anyone or anything completely figured out, I've got myself and the whole world out of perspective.

When I speak in "God Almighty" statements, I leave you no room to wiggle. I'll give you a horrible example, directly out of my experience. Several years ago when I was still fighting for the establishment's line on long hair, I looked over at my teenage son. He was sitting in a chair and looking out the window, his hair slightly below the top of his shirt collar and beginning to curl up at the ends. A sudden rush of frustration and anger went through me and I said, "Bobby, that is the most effeminate looking head of hair I have ever seen on a male in my life!" (A "God Almighty" statement if I ever uttered one!)

Not a muscle moved on my son's face, nor did his gaze shift from whatever was (or was not) claiming his attention out the window. What *could* he say? What could he *do*? The pronouncement had come from on high, at least from Mount Olympus. How do you fight against God? It's futile. Better not to get involved. He was wise; he didn't.

After about thirty seconds I said something else. I don't know why I said it, but I did. Perhaps the inauthenticity of what I had said became evident even then, before I knew about "God Almighty" statements. It was redemptive. I said, "Or so it seems to me." With that my son swung around in his chair, looked me square in the eye, smiled (I swear to God he smiled), and said, "I'm sorry you feel that way."

My second comment had cracked the "God Almightiness" of the first one. It opened up the possibility for some communication between mortals. I will speak at greater length in the next chapter about the alternative to "God Almighty" statements. My point now is this: A "God Almighty" statement automatically destroys the possibility of communication. Usually it is received as an accusation against which a person must defend himself or herself. It treats the one to whom it is addressed as something other than an authentic human being.

I am convinced this is one main reason much of our conversation involves "God Almighty" statements. Often, whether we're aware of it or not, we don't want a response, or at least something strong within us doesn't want one. To engage a person in honest communication is to risk finding ourselves wrong. We would have to accept personal responsibility for what we think and feel. To communicate openly is to admit the possibility of discovering some things about ourselves we don't want to know. It would allow the other person to be who he or she is, rather than what we want him or her to be.

Recently I was talking with a woman whose husband of thirteen years had walked out on her the week before. She explained that their relationship had been tense for a couple of years and had grown progressively worse. Several times she had suggested going to see a marriage counselor, but her husband refused. Finally, she had all she could take. She told him, "Either we see a counselor or I'm through!" Her husband packed up and moved out, leaving her and the three kids behind.

Now she may have been right. The assistance of a marriage counselor may have been just what they needed, but coming at her husband in this way left him no room to wiggle. Had he relented and agreed to see a counselor, it would have been the same as saying, "You're right and have been all along. It's my stubbornness that has allowed this marriage to get in the mess it's in today. I am a dirty, bad, stupid person." Now nobody wants to say that, even if he thinks it, perhaps *especially* if he thinks it. The way his wife approached her husband left him no dignified way out except to get out, and he did.

As I talked with this lady, I discovered that she had lots of mixed feelings about the whole situation. We always do, about everything. But she began to see that she really could not say with absolute certainty that a marriage counselor was the *only* possible hope for their marriage. It *seemed* to her that it was, but that isn't what she said. Would it have made any difference if she had phrased it differently? Nobody knows. But what she really meant could have been said in such a way as to give her husband more options. It could have been said so that he could have responded with whatever interest he may have had in preserving the marriage. It's just possible that he had some ideas for working on the marriage but never got an opportunity to get them out.

We complain, "No one understands me," but for all our yearning to be understood, something within us doesn't want to be understood. If you understood me, really understood me, you probably wouldn't like or respect me. At least I fear you wouldn't. You would know how frightened I get sometimes. You would know how often I bluff when I don't have the slightest idea of what I'm talking about. You would discover that I am, frankly, unsure of some of the things about which I speak most emphatically. If you really understood me, you would know how much I want to be right and how much I fear I'm wrong. It would become apparent to you that I'm afraid I don't matter very much, and that's the last thing I want you to know. *I want to matter!* Oh, how I want to matter! But if I let you know me, I probably won't matter to you at all.

So what do I do? When I get in a tight and when I feel that I am ineffective and powerless, I speak to you in "God Almighty" statements. I reach for some outside authority to bolster my eroding confidence. I give you no opportunity for an authentic response. That way, I keep the game going. You don't understand me. I'm wearing the guise of omnipotence. I don't understand you. It's all frustrating and anxiety-producing, but it's better (at least, it seems so at the moment) than running the horrible risk of letting my fears be known.

And yet there are times, often late at night when the weight in my stomach and the lump in my throat and the buzzing in my brain won't let me sleep, when I wish with all my might that somebody could understand me! But no one can understand me unless I'm willing to allow my real self to be known—to say what I mean.

2

"I FEEL" STATEMENTS

How many times have you heard a parent wail to a teenage child or a miserable wife plead-complain to her husband, "I feel as if I don't know you any more"? It happens all the time, and for good reason. We can never know anyone, not in any deep, personal way, unless that person chooses to disclose himself or herself to us.

When a teenager retreats to his room, responds politely or impolitely to questions, and volunteers no information about "how it is" with him the parent is going to feel left out, frightened, and in the dark—and he is.

You could follow me around for months, take voluminous notes on my habits, activities, and conversations, and still not know me. At the end of that time you would know a great deal *about* me, but you wouldn't know me. You can know me only as I choose to allow you to know what I hope and fear in the depths of my being.

If you were to know me, you would have to know the

profound loneliness I feel when I appear brave, the deep sadness inhabiting me sometimes when I'm acting carefree, the yearning for friendship overwhelming me at some of those moments when I'm being so hard to get along with. Knowing me would include knowing my personal value system, the one that actually determines my life, not necessarily the one I defend in public. You can't know any of this unless I tell you.

Unless I allow you to know me, you have no choice but to treat me on the basis of what you see in me or, what happens more often, on the basis of your reaction to what you see in me. When you do this, I'm not going to feel understood. In fact, it is likely that I will feel terribly misunderstood. That isn't me. If you are to know me and if there is to be authentic communication between us, I must dare to risk letting you know how I feel.

This, therefore, is the alternative to "God Almighty" statements. If we are willing to put an "I Feel" in front of our "God Almighty" statements, they become authentic expressions of who we are and where we are. If I give you an "I Feel" statement, you have the opportunity to respond to me and not to some puffed-up caricature of me. At first glance this may seem a weak-kneed, inhibiting way to talk, but it's just the opposite. When I am willing to put an "I Feel" in front of my statement, I can say anything, and no one can challenge my accuracy. They may disagree; that possibility is wide open. But at least they are disagreeing with me and not with some intellectual abstraction. The possibility for real, personal communication now exists.

This approach to communication came to me in the midst of a counseling situation and in light of a passage in the Sermon on the Mount which I was studying at the time. It worked well for the family with whom I was talking. The more I thought about it, the more of an "Aha!" experience it seemed. So I talked to more people about it, and they found it helpful also. My excitement grew. The time had come to unload it on my most crucial audience—my family. Would you believe it? They weren't interested. It seems they had heard too many of Dad's bright ideas before; so after a day or two of trying to convince them, I gave up—with them, anyway.

Then two or three months later something happened that still represents the classic example of this system's worth—and it happened in my family.

It was a Sunday. We were to have a New Member Orientation at our home that afternoon at four o'clock. At the dinner table I explained to all the kids (we have four) that it would be necessary for them to get their rooms cleaned up before the guests arrived. About three o'clock I made my inspection.

All rooms had been cleaned except one, Dianne's. Of our four kids Dianne is normally the most orderly. I blew my top. I screamed for Dianne to get her fanny off the couch and up those stairs in a hurry.

When she arrived, I let her have it. "Dianne, this is the messiest room I have ever seen in my entire life!"

That twelve-year-old demon-angel looked me right in the eye, hard as nails, and said, "Daddy, that sounds like a "God Almighty" statement to me!"

That really did it! I mean that *really* did it! Not only had my explicit instructions been disobeyed, my own "system," ignored for months, was being thrown back in my face. Words cannot express the fury with which I said through tightly clenched teeth, "*I feel* this is the messiest room I have ever seen in my life!"

But then the "system" began to function. In spite of my rage, as soon as I said, "*I feel* this is the messiest room I have ever seen in my life," I knew it wasn't true. That was not what I was feeling. At the moment, I didn't know what I was feeling, but obviously that wasn't it. So I had to take it back. That's one of the rules and one of the options. If your "I Feel" statement doesn't ring authentic, you can take it back and try another.

As nearly as I can recall, I had to take four or five cracks at it before I got to an authentic "I Feel" statement. After several attempts, I finally managed, "I feel that I must not be very important to you since you disregarded what I asked you to do." Something inside me said, "That rings true. That is what you're feeling." So I said to Dianne, "That's it. That's how I feel."

You know what she said? "Daddy, I really do understand. I probably would feel that way about it too. In fact, there have been some times when I have felt like I wasn't very important to you."

Now words escape me. How can I describe the beauty of that moment? I hadn't even understood myself at the outset, and yet I was being understood by my twelve-year-old daughter—understood and *accepted*. What's more, she not only understood me, she was willing to give some of her authentic feelings to me. I was able to understand and accept them—to understand and accept *her*. I could only take her in my arms and weep for joy.

I am just authoritarian enough to have been through plenty of similar situations before. I know how they go and how this one would have gone if Dianne had not had what it takes to call me on my "God Almighty" statement. Sulking, she would have gone into her room and cleaned it up. I would have walked away feeling perfectly justified but miserable. I don't enjoy being at swords' points with those I love. For a couple of days we would have gone on living in the same house but with nothing more communicative to say to each other than a hard-lipped "Please pass the butter." Instead, we had one of the most beautiful moments life has to offer, a moment of personal understanding and acceptance between a father and his daughter. I decided it was worth writing a book about.

The more I think about it, the more convinced I become that "God Almighty" statements are actually "I Feel" statements in disguise. Much as they appear to state rational facts, "God Almighty" statements spring from feeling. Now I may or may not be aware of what that feeling is myself, but in either case it is a feeling which is not expressed for what it is. It is a feeling in disguise. More than likely, most "God Almighty" statements are trying to say, "I would like to have more attention than I am getting," or "I wish you loved me as much as I love you," or "Sometimes I feel as if no one listens to me at all," or "I wish you could know how frightened I get when you do or don't do that," or "Won't somebody pay attention to me?"

To make an "I Feel" statement is to say what you mean without disguise. When you get in the habit of making "I Feel" statements, you can relax a bit. You don't have to be so careful that your wording is "just right." Once you've said it, if it doesn't sound authentic, you can take it back and have another go at it. It's exciting to get at your real feeling. You learn a lot of things about yourself, many of them good.

"I Feel" statements also allow you to feel more authentic about yourself. You will be relieved of those agonizing situations in which you find yourself pretending—pretending you are an expert in something you don't really know that much about, pretending you never make a mistake, pretending you still think you are right after it has become clearly evident even to you that you are mistaken.

But simply putting an "I Feel" in front of your "God Almighty" statement doesn't necessarily make it an authentic "I Feel" statement, at least not as it stands. What usually happens is that when you hear yourself make your "God Almighty" statement with the "I Feel" in front, its inauthenticity becomes evident. You can take it back, saying, "No, that's not it." You are permitted another go at it, and then another, until you have gotten down to the real feeling.

Putting the "I Feel" in front gets us started on becoming aware of our real feeling. Only when we are in touch with our feelings do we begin really to know ourselves. And only when we know at least something of who we really are can we let our real selves be known. If others are ever to understand us, we must be aware and allow them to know us. How can anyone understand us unless we are willing to tell that person how it is with us, who we really are?

When we quit trying to masquerade as God (which is what we're doing when we make "God Almighty" statements), we discover how much more fun and relaxing it is to be human. It takes a lot of pressure off, the pressure of an impossible burden—knowing everything, always being right, never making a mistake. Instead of trying to manipulate other people (which is the objective of our "God Almighty" statements whether we recognize it as such or not), we can begin to enjoy them and ourselves.

Suddenly it begins to be possible for us to tell other people who we are. In the process, we ourselves discover more and more about who we are. That's really exciting. You might even learn to like yourself. In fact, I am convinced that if you will try the "I Feel" way of life, you will learn to like yourself. I believe God has made every one of us somebody special, well worth knowing.

Making "I Feel" statements leaves the other person the opportunity for response. He or she can say "I'm sorry you feel that way," as my son did in the example I cited in the first chapter, or "I understand why you feel that way," as my daughter did in the messy-room episode. Or the other person can say a whole myriad of other things. He or she has room to wiggle and is free to respond with an "I Feel" statement. That's the beginning of authentic, human communication.

When I come at a person with an "I Feel" instead of a "God Almighty," I not only make a more accurate representation of who I am, allowing him or her to know who I am, I also give the other person the dignity of being an authentic human being. I don't speak as if all the wisdom in God's creation is stored in my cranium. I allow for the possibility that he or she may also have something of worth to say on this subject. Most people like being treated with dignity. I do. That other person is much more likely to give you a civil response when he or she feels respectfully treated. Instead of fighting in a futile effort to prove somebody right and somebody wrong, the stage is set for growth, insight, and honest encounter between two authentic human beings, and real life happens.

3

WHY CAN'T WE JUST TALK?

If "God Almighty" statements are destructive and usually achieve the opposite of what we're seeking, why do we keep making them? Allowing for individual differences of personality and style, it seems to me there is one basic reason we persist in using "God Almighty" statements: We have a deep and nagging fear that we do not matter.

Drawing on the sensitivity to human life which made him an award-winning novelist and on his experiences in the apartheid society of his native South Africa, Alan Paton wrote in the *Saturday Review of Literature:*

> How does one help ordinary men and women, if not to eliminate fear, at least to keep it within bounds, so that reason may play a stronger role in the affairs of men and nations and so that men may cease to pursue policies which must lead to the disasters they fear? *To me, this is the most important question that confronts the human race.*[1]

1. Alan Paton, "The Challenge of Fear," *Saturday Review of Literature*, 9 September 1967, p. 20, italics mine.

In his best-seller, *I'm OK—You're OK*, psychiatrist Thomas A. Harris draws on medical and psychological studies to come to the same conclusion. He contends that everyone in the world, at or around age two, makes a decision about himself: I'm not OK; you are OK. Tragically, most people never make another deeply authentic decision about themselves for the rest of their lives. As a consequence, they operate out of the "not OK" pocket. One way or another they are seeking to gain affirmation from the "OK" authority figures in their lives. That, I think, is why we make "God Almighty" statements. We want to matter and fear we don't. Our pseudocertainty and phony confidence is a futile effort to prove that we do.

Does this make sense in your experience? Doesn't the bully push people around in an effort to get attention? Isn't the little high-school girl eager to go steady to prove that she is somebody special? Aren't teenagers likely to do a lot of crazy things to get acceptance from their peers? Is it really the money that keeps a businessman working like a dog? Then why isn't he satisfied when he reaches what has always been his goal? What is the impetus behind the women's liberation movement? Don't women want to be recognized as persons of unique and independent worth?

Every one of us longs to know that he or she matters, and each of us is deeply fearful that he or she does not. The more arrogant and cocksure a person is, the greater the likelihood that he or she is terribly afraid.

Check the sources of conflict in your life. If you probe to the depths, what do you find?

Those times when I am most miserable, when I have the biggest knot in my stomach and the most unrelenting despair in my head, are when something has happened that makes me look like a failure and a fool. If I feel that way about myself, what do others think? I have done a less than satisfactory job in my profession. My kids have acted in such a way as to make it appear I'm not much of a parent. Someone on whom I had counted for love and support has let me down. I have done some dumb thing that shatters a favorite self-image. Whatever it may have been, the end result is that the thing I fear most seems to be confirmed: I appear to me to be a person who doesn't matter.

Why do husbands and wives fight with each other? My experience indicates that most marital fights, whatever they may *seem* to be about, are really about one thing, namely, "You have hurt my feelings. What you did or didn't do makes me feel as if I don't matter." Hurt feelings are seldom what people *talk about* in a marital fight, but beneath all the hostile rhetoric, that's what's usually going on.

A man is on his way out the door in the morning. His wife calls out, "Whatever you do, don't forget to pick up my coat at the cleaners." Well, the husband has one of those days. He's so busy making new deals and patching up old ones that he doesn't even have time for lunch. When he finally gets home, congratulating himself for not being too late for the party they're going to that night, he's forgotten the coat. His wife is furious, not so much for the coat she isn't able to wear (although that's all she talks about), but because her husband's failure to pick it up makes it appear that she doesn't matter to him as much as his business.

The husband feels sorry and a little guilty, but he also experiences himself as horribly misunderstood! Does she think he enjoys putting himself through that rat race every day? Why does she think he works so hard if it's not for her and the kids? He's knocking himself out to do something for the family, and all she can think about is a coat that didn't get picked up. What this says to him is that he and his effort don't matter very much. So they berate each other with vindictive accusations. Neither really feels any better for it, but it seemed necessary to preserve their dignity and honor.

Far from being a deeply subtle insight, this need to retaliate is so obvious that education and sophistication may serve only to obscure it. Not long ago I was having a premarital counseling conference. The groom-to-be was a man in his early forties. This was his second marriage. After his divorce, some eight or nine years before, he resolved never to marry again. But he met this girl, and they had been dating for two years. She wanted to get married. He loved her, so why not? This was his explanation, just as simple, honest, and straightforward as that.

I was talking to them, as I always do in these conferences, about the importance of communication. I explained that often we don't say what we mean but make "God Almighty" statements instead and get "God Almighty" statements in return. I wasn't sure I was getting through, but the man spoke up. His comment made me realize I was being understood perfectly. In fact, he gave me one of the most marvelously unsophisticated examples of how we react to our hurt feelings rather than communicating that I have ever heard.

"Just yesterday," he said, "we were driving along when she said to me, 'Those cars up in front of you are slowing down.' And I said, 'Yeah, and it takes you two hours to make spaghetti, but it still comes out cold.' " The man understood perfectly what I was saying about dishonest communication. When she threatened his image of himself, he immediately went to work to attack hers.

What about conflict between parents and children? Some things are important to parents—values and lifestyles that represent security and the meaning of life to them. Their lives are built on them. The collapse of their structure is a personal tragedy. When kids act as if school doesn't matter and good manners don't matter and going to church doesn't matter, parents take this personally. It seems to them that the kids are saying, "You don't matter!" Because that is precisely the fear the parents are carrying around in their tummies (though often unrecognized), the actions of their kids fall right on the most sensitive spot.

In an effort to reassert that they do matter (like, "Please, God, let me matter!"), parents begin making "God Almighty" demands. "Do this, or else!" Or else what? That's not always clear, but to the kids it often seems that to capitulate is to surrender what little sense of worth they may possess. To "give in" would be to "give up." So, in a determined effort to prove that they do matter, kids defy their parents even more vigorously. And the gap widens all because everyone needs to feel that he matters and is scared to death that he doesn't.

What about racial conflict? The racial revolution began in America right after World War II. Military mobilization moved many young blacks out of their restricted environments and into areas of life they never dreamed existed. With the advent of television, the "American way of life" began to be pumped into both mansions and shacks all over the country on a daily basis. It began to occur to black persons that they might live their whole lives through and never have lived the "real thing" at all. That's pretty frightening, to live and never to have lived at all. So they began making demands. They wanted to know they mattered. They insisted on their share of the goodies.

To the whites this was a threat to what made them matter. They had been taught to assume "Everyone knows it's better to be white than black." But now they were hearing "Black is beautiful." If it ever got going that it's just as good to be black as to be white, the whites would have lost something that gives them a sense of mattering: the superiority of being white. So whites began to resist. The more they resisted, the more the black people pushed. The conflict got hotter, all because everyone needs to know he matters and fears he does not!

Even if you are willing to agree that this fear is near the core of most life-conflicts, you may wonder what it has to do with the ability to communicate. The answer is *everything!* One of the biggest instances of this fear is that we are afraid to let others know how fearful we are. Since this fear that we don't matter is part of everything we do, unless we are willing to acknowledge our fear, no one will ever understand us.

A number of years ago a couple whom I had known well came to see me. They were winsome, intelligent people, married for about eighteen years, active in the church and the community, well liked by everyone. They came in to tell me they were getting a divorce. I'm beyond the point of shock, but I was surprised.

"There's no sense kidding around about this with you, Bob," he said. "She's just a frigid wench, and I can't stand it any more."

"If we're going to put it all out on the table," said she, "he's a sex maniac, and there's no way that anyone could ever satisfy him."

They had me convinced. That seemed to be the brutal bottom of it. But they continued to talk for a few minutes, and then the husband said, "You know, sometimes it scares me that I can't turn her on any more than I do. It makes me afraid that I must not be much of a man."

His wife who had previously reported that not a kind word had been exchanged between them for months, reached over and put her hand tenderly on top of his. "Scared?" she said. "It never once occurred to me that you might be scared. You go roaring around the house like a wounded water buffalo. Scared is what I am. I've tried and tried to be the kind of wife you want me to be, and I can't do it. I'm scared to death that I'm just not an adequate woman."

They had finally gotten to what was really going on: They were both afraid they didn't matter. Their problems didn't end on the spot, but it was the first giant step toward a reconciliation. At last report they were doing fine, better than ever before. How sad that two fine people had to spend so many years making themselves and each other miserable because they had been afraid to make an "I Feel" statement, to tell each other their fear. For the moment, at least, that was the most real thing they had to share; and, as it turns out, it was the one thing they had most in common.

"I'm not afraid of anything." Bah! We're all afraid we don't matter. That's why we can't "just talk."

That's why the bully is a bully. He's afraid that someone might find out how frightened he is, that he doesn't matter, that he might never be noticed, that he might be just as insignificant as he feels. That's why the "wallflower" is a "wallflower." She fears that if she ever opened her mouth all her scared feelings might come pouring out. Then everyone would know how ignorant and incapable she feels. So she keeps it all clammed up, yearning for someone who will know, understand, and appreciate her but never giving anyone the chance.

People who look terribly different are, in this respect, very much alike. Some people react to crisis by "overcontrolling." That's what I tend to do. I come home, find the place in an uproar, kids running everywhere, coats and books thrown in every direction. I take over. I start making like God Almighty: "You do this; you do that; put this there; put that somewhere else." It's a reaction to fear. The messy house has made me feel as if I'm not in charge of what's happening in my own home. That scares me, so I try to control everything.

Some people react just the opposite to the same kind of crisis. They run away and hide. They shut their eyes and ears and minds to the problem. They hope "it" will go away. From the outside they look so different from us "controllers," but it's the same thing. They just respond differently. It's a reaction to fear. We can shout and scream at one another (as I have been known to do) about the best way to handle a situation, but that doesn't accomplish a thing. Why can't we tell one another the truth?

"The truth is that I'm afraid. This thing really scares me."

"You, too? Man, that's what it does to me."

"I guess we'd better take a look at our fears then, right?"

"Right. Maybe we don't need to be so afraid. Maybe we can help each other."

If we're going to communicate, we need to learn to talk about our fears. They're at the core of who we are and where we are. Alan Paton has it right.

If only a man would say, "I do this because I'm afraid," one could bear it; but when he says, "I do this because I'm good," that is a bit too much.[2]

_____
2. Ibid., p. 21.

4

WHAT IT TAKES TO TURN AROUND

If we were all to agree that fear is the problem, what could we do about it? There's a little line tucked away near the end of the New Testament (1 John 4:18) which, it seems to me, is at the heart of the gospel and is the key to man's most pressing problem: "Perfect love casts out fear." This strikes me as the one authentic way to gain assurance that we matter. We know we matter when we discover we are important to some other person, and we begin to grow when we believe that some other person cares about us.

We may not be any more eager for love to be the answer than we are for fear to be the problem. Both exist beyond our invention and control. Even so, you can hardly but marvel at the remarkable healing power of a mother's kiss. A child gets a finger caught in a car door. There is, of course, real physical pain, but apparently that isn't the essence of the problem. If it were, how could mother's kissing the injured pinky bring relief? Perhaps the deeper pain is terror.

The child has seen that car door close many times. He knows there isn't room for a finger in there in the midst of all that hard metal, but the impossible happened, and it hurts! What kind of world is this where freakish, impossible, painful things happen? Haven't we all, of whatever age, asked ourselves that question? How can a person feel safe living in such an unpredictable, uncontrollable world?

The child comes to mother. She is sympathetic, but what has happened doesn't terrify her. The child trusts mother, and mother seems confident that everything is going to be OK. The fear begins to fade, and with the fear goes much of the pain. It's the same for all of us. When we can get our fears out of the way, we are able to cope with life's problems for what they really are. He was exaggerating, I think, but President Franklin D. Roosevelt's point is well taken. In his first inaugural address, he told the American people. "The only thing we have to fear is fear itself." Fear immobilizes us; it prevents our doing what we are able to do.

I've seen it happen hundreds of times in a dozen different forms. A teenager goes along, sometimes up but more often down. To hear him talk, you'd get the impression that life is pretty stinking. Then he falls in love, and everything changes. I've even been told, quite confidentially, that when you start going steady you can even handle solid geometry! What's the connection? Well, as I see it, this makes just as much sense as the small child's hurt finger and his mother's kiss, and for the same reason. When you know someone loves you, you can handle life. Your fears about not mattering and all the pain and turmoil that go with them are dissolved in the overwhelming wonder of being loved.

If the fear that we do not matter is at the center of our

sickness, then the assurance of personal love must be the most important medicine in the whole world.

Isn't that the real thrill of having a friend, of dating and necking, of getting married, of having someone to come home to and to hold you? Here is a person who, in spite of all the doubts and fears I have about myself, thinks I'm important. This person cares about me. The world is alive with the singing of birds and the sound of poetry! O happy day! I am loved! I don't have to be afraid any more. I matter!

The crucial place that love occupies in our lives is precisely what makes all substitutes unsatisfactory. I'm not about to knock the ego-boosting benefits of being elected president of the senior class or being chosen homecoming queen or making the winning touchdown on Thanksgiving Day or bringing home straight A's or water-skiing or landing the biggest contract ever handled by your firm or being chosen president of the PTA. I would venture to ask, however, "How thrilling would these things be if no one else ever knew about them?" Back in my day a popular ballad said, "If no one shares and no one cares, where's the joy in a job well done?"

Achievements are important, but the disappointing thing is that the confidence born of them doesn't last long. If you get a new surge of self-worth by today's accomplishments, what are you going to do tomorrow? If achievements are the basis for your confidence, you've got to keep achieving. It gets tiring.

Have you ever seen a fellow trying to convince his friends what a big man he was the day he went a hundred yards for a touchdown? It's sad. No one cares any more. You keep hearing stories about successful businessmen and movie stars who jump out of high office buildings or take an overdose of sleeping pills. How come life seems so hopeless to them if they are so successful? Apparently, the one thing that lets us know we matter had eluded them. It would appear that what makes life worth living is not found in what we normally call "success."

We know we matter when we know that someone loves us, and that love is what we keep trying to get through other means. We keep looking for that assurance in business, recreation, fancy clothes, ratty clothes, sex, and all the rest, but it doesn't come that way—not really. Admitting, as I'm more than willing to do, that kissing is a lot of fun, it has to be more than the touch of lips on lips that sends a teenage boy right out of his gourd. What thrills him to the depths of his soul is the assurance that some live human being, who doesn't have to, thinks he's special.

Sexual expression that does not carry with it the assurance of personal worth is a great disappointment. What we're looking for, I believe, is not sex but an authentic, personal experience that we matter. That's why so much sex, both inside and outside marriage, is disappointing. It is much easier to "make love" than it is to make a relationship, and the relationship in which we discover we matter is the only thing that satisfies our deepest need.

That's one big reason there are frustrated marriages. For so many people, marriage becomes a jungle of disappointed expectations. They had counted on it heavily. Being married was going to make so many wrong things right. All of us go into marriage with certain expectations, both conscious and unconscious. It almost never turns out that way. One would hope that the realities would be even better than the expectations, but in any event marriage is seldom exactly as we had imagined it. So, for a time at least, we are filled with disappointment. Then the disappointment turns to resentment. "I'm being cheated. He's (she's) holding out on me."

Didn't she stand there in her white wedding gown, in front of God, mommy and daddy, and a whole host of her friends and say, "I'm going to spend 100 percent of my time letting you know that you matter"? Well, that's not exactly what she said, but that's how he interpreted it.

As it turns out, she was expecting the same thing. Of course, neither one would have said it. It may not even have occurred to them in words, but chances are that both of them were expecting marriage to be somewhere near the end of all their doubts. If a woman is willing to commit herself to love me for the rest of my life, surely I will never again have to worry about whether or not I matter. That should settle it, once and for all, but it doesn't. It seems that she was expecting the same thing, that I would spend 100 percent of my time loving her. With both of us so eager to be loved, that doesn't leave much of anyone around to do any loving. So we're both disappointed, and our feelings are hurt, and we're still afraid we don't matter—only more so, because the one thing on which we had counted has melted out from under us.

One of the feelings that follows is "You're making a fool of me! Here I am all hung out on loving you, and you don't even seem to care!" Now we really don't want anyone making a fool of us. We feel foolish enough as it is, all by ourselves. So when we feel the love we want so much slipping away and then turning into hostility, we have to fight that person. He or she is taking our life away.

There are lots of ways to fight. The frontal attack is just one, and not even the most common. You can fight by pouting, by dropping smiling-but-sarcastic comments on your spouse's weakest point (after you've lived with someone for a while, you know what those points are), by spending more and more time away from home, by refusing to listen seriously to what is said, by getting totally involved with the kids or bridge or golf or church work or a profession.

Usually, these efforts are not simply ways of "getting

back." Somewhere in the background, consciously or unconsciously, they are usually attempts to manipulate the other person into giving you the love you want and need so desperately. Who hasn't spent some time mapping out a strategy for getting a specific reaction? All the way from cooking his favorite meal, so he will be in the right mood, to making his life so miserable that he will beg for mercy, to being so quietly sweet and loving that he will have to repent. There are hundreds, maybe thousands, of ways we can work out for making that other person love us the way we want to be loved.

The tragedy is that none of them works. Even if one of them *seems* to work, it doesn't. Even if he responds *exactly* as you had hoped (don't count on it), *you* know it is a manipulated response. That isn't what we're looking for. What you and I want so desperately is someone who will love us because he or she has chosen to love us. If the expression of love is simply the result of our calculated scheming, or even if we *think* it is, the assurance that we matter isn't there. We want a free response, but we're afraid to let the other person be free to respond as he or she will. We don't have that much confidence in the other person or in ourselves. We have been hurt too often before.

It's a pretty hopeless feeling. More than I need anything else, I need to know that I matter. The only way I know I matter is for someone to love me, but there's no way I can *make* anyone love me. If I coax or coerce another into giving me expressions of love, it's phony and I know it. I end up feeling even worse. What's a person to do?

I am convinced that the only way we can get love is by believing it. The answer is *faith.* That's what it takes to turn around.

Just in case you are hung up about religion having easy but irrelevant answers to everything, let me slip a word in here from Erich Fromm, one of the most widely respected psychotherapists in the world. His classic book, *The Art of Loving,* has been selling thousands of copies for years, all over the world. Fromm goes to great pains in this book to make it clear that he doesn't need any God in his system. I find this interesting since he quotes and interprets Scripture throughout the book and since near the end, when he starts clinching his argument, he quotes extensively from the words of Jesus Christ.

Be that as it may, and I really have no credentials for analyzing this master analyst, Fromm has no doubts at all about what it takes to make a life of love possible.

> This process of emergence, of birth, or waking up, requires one quality as a necessary condition: *faith*. The practice of the art of loving requires the practice of faith.[1]

If I cannot believe that I am loved and capable of loving, in spite of how much to the opposite it often *seems* to me, then I will not be able to receive love or give it. That's why no one can ever prove to me that he or she loves me. No matter how tenaciously I may demand proof, no matter how valiantly and incessantly he or she may try to give it, either I believe it or I don't get it.

Years ago, a pretty high-school girl came to see me with a tale of woe. It has proven to be such a classic that I'm sure I'll never forget it. She and Robert had been going "steadily" for some time. Rachel (that's what we'll call her) was putting the pressure on for them to go steady, but Robert's folks were against it. Rachel kept after it. She told Robert that if they could just go steady everything would be fine. He didn't have to give her his letter sweater or class ring (that's what steadies did in those days) if he would just assure her that they were going steady. So Robert relented. For a while, everything was beautiful.

Then Rachel, as she admitted, began to feel uncomfort-

---

1. Erich Fromm, *The Art of Loving* (New York: Harper & Bros., 1956), p. 121.

able. All the other girls who were going steady had some evidence of their status. Why couldn't Robert let her have his class ring? Robert relented again. She got the ring, and again, for a while, everything was OK; but it turns out that wasn't enough either.

Rachel's best friend, Robin, had a steady, Richard. Richard called Robin on the phone every single night of the world. "How come," Rachel said to Robert, "if you love me as much as Richard loves Robin, you don't call me every night?" Good old Robert. He started calling Rachel every night, and you know what Rachel said to him when he did? "You wouldn't be calling me if I hadn't asked you to."

If you're not Rachel, this whole episode is pretty funny, but one way or another, we are all Rachel. We keep demanding love of the people who are important to us, and then, even if they give it, we don't believe it. Remember, as far as love is concerned, if you don't believe it, you don't get it, no matter how much love may be out there for you.

Faith in what? What am I supposed to believe in order to get the love I want and need? Well, just for starters, we need to believe we are lovable. That's hard to do, especially in view of the fact that ever since you were two years old you've been believing you are "not OK." But if you can't believe you are lovable, how are you ever going to believe you are loved?

A second thing you need to believe is that you are capable of loving. Perhaps you've never even thought about that, but I run into it, literally, all the time. There's nothing I see more consistently in people who have been through a divorce, even one that is called a "friendly divorce." To have failed in life's most important human relationship is bound to raise doubts, not only as to whether or not I am loved, but as to whether or not I am capable of loving.

Divorced persons aren't the only ones. I know lots of

married people who are scared to death that they don't have what it takes to maintain a love relationship over any extended period of time. Maybe they came out of unhappy, loveless homes. Whatever the reason, if persons do not have confidence in their ability to love, they will not be able to give themselves to a vital love relationship.

Which brings us to a third thing we need to believe: I can reveal myself without being destroyed. In his recent book, *I Ain't Much, Baby—But I'm All I've Got*, Jess Lair has a neat definition of love. It's not the last word on the subject, and maybe it's not even the best definition available, but it's new and helpful. He says, "Love is when we tell what's in our deepest hearts." [2] I can only let someone know how it is with me in my deepest heart if I have faith that to make such a vulnerable revelation will not destroy me.

But how am I to get this faith? Well, you can't get it unless you experience it, and I'm convinced that love is all around us if we are willing to open ourselves to experience it. There is also a lot of hostility and hate, but each of us has to decide: Which is the most authentic and real indication of who I am? The hostility that some people give off toward me, or the love that some people express to me? You'll never know unless you open yourself to find out.

That is one reason Lair's definition charms me so. If you want love, he tells you what you can do to find it. Open yourself. Put yourself in a vulnerable position. Make an "I Feel" statement. Let someone know how it is with you in your deepest heart. Then if there is any love out there waiting for you, you'll find it.

But once you've experienced it, you have to believe it. You have to take it inside and make it a part of you. That's hard to do. Many old images are tucked away inside telling you how "not OK" you are, but, as Dr. Harris

---

2. Jess Lair, *I Ain't Much, Baby—But I'm All I've Got* (Garden City, N.Y.: Doubleday, 1972), p. 37.

says in his book, you have to decide whether you are what you've always thought or whether you are what this new here-and-now experience of love says you are. The decision is crucial. Hang on to the old image, and you're stuck. Risk accepting a new image of yourself, and you admit the possibility of a whole new kind of life. You become a different person when you believe you are loved.

Faking it won't work. Either you believe it or you don't—except, of course, I seriously doubt that any of us has perfect faith. What I mean is, when some guy goes around always slapping people on the back, seeming so completely confident, you may pick up bad vibrations from him. You may get the feeling that he is trying to tell you how great you are in the hope that you, in response, will turn around and tell him how great he is. You never know how many buckets of tears that guy may cry when he's alone in his room at night. So far as love is concerned, either you believe it or you don't get it. There just isn't any other way.

5

THE FEAR OF FEELING

We don't want fear to be the problem, so we have to pretend the problem is something else. For example, a schoolteacher is having fits with a particular boy in her class. She keeps complaining to the principal about what a troublemaker the boy is. Finally, the principal takes the boy out of her class. That should solve the problem, but before long the teacher comes up with another troublemaker.

The teacher has to have a scapegoat; otherwise she would be forced to look into herself. She would have to face some of her own fears that are contributing to the tension. Since that's too threatening, she finds herself another troublemaker. Then, when she gets home at night all tired and discouraged, she can just say, "If it weren't for that boy, my life would be beautiful. It's his fault I'm so miserable."

Having heard hundreds of couples talk about their problems, I am convinced that nearly all marital fights have one subject: hurt feelings. You can say it in a number of ways. Perhaps I should mention a few:

"You make me feel like I don't matter."

"You don't seem to care about me as much as I care about you."

"Who I am and what I feel are not important to you."

"You don't understand me and won't even try."

However you say it, it all revolves around hurt feelings. But in our fighting we hardly ever get to the hurt feelings. In other words, hurt feelings are at the core of 100 percent of our marital fights, but that's what we talk about only, say, 2 percent of the time. The rest of the time we talk about sex, money, rearing the kids, in-laws, being on time, keeping a clean house, drinking, not drinking, and stuff like that. I'm not saying these things are unimportant. They just aren't what the fight is really about.

And that is why most marital fights never get anywhere. *We seldom get around to talking about what the fight is about.* We don't say what we mean. Since we don't say what it's about, perhaps don't even know, how can we possibly resolve it? Saying what we mean wouldn't eliminate all the hurt feelings or fighting, but it would put them in a place where they could be dealt with constructively and creatively.

The statistics are that sex is the leading cause of divorce in America. I think that's a bum rap for sex. The way I look at it, sex problems are usually not sex problems at all. They are problems in communication, of not being understood, of feeling used or cheated—in other words, hurt feelings. Many of our hurt feelings seem to land on sex because it is such a sensitive indicator of how we feel about ourselves and the other person. If a man has hurt feelings toward his wife, regardless of where they come from, those feelings are bound to show up in a destructive way in the personal sensitivity and closeness of the sexual relationship.

He gets mad because sex is no good, but if he then concludes that the problem is sex, he has missed the boat. What's wrong is the hurt feelings between him and his wife. Unless they can recognize and talk about them, they'll never get at what's going on.

Undoubtedly, rational thinking has made possible the amazing American standard of life, and I'm grateful. But rational thinking has its drawbacks, and one is the felt necessity to reduce everything to a rational, definable equation. It makes us uncomfortable if we cannot say, "That's the problem and this is the answer!" We feel weak, inadequate, and helpless, something less than straight-thinking American citizens.

If we cannot reduce our troubles to a definable, rational problem, we experience being "out of control." If our human relationships cannot be explained in purely rational terms, we are stuck with dealing with feelings. That makes us uncomfortable. Feelings are dangerous and explosive. Feelings will not easily submit to mechanical analysis and management. We seem convinced that feelings will get us in trouble.

Why is it so hard to admit and cope with feelings? Why do we seem determined to define our problems in other terms? Just for starters, you might consider that in many ways our society teaches us to suppress our feelings. If a little boy falls off his bike and skins his knee, he is quickly reminded that "big boys don't cry." We order little girls to kiss Aunt Susie good-bye because we love her so much when, in fact, Aunt Susie has acted like a police-dog monster to the little girl the whole weekend.

I'm not taking potshots at anyone. I've done more than my share of repressing feelings and blaming my problems on someone else. I can remember times when I'd use my day off to take the kids somewhere special, like to a circus. I'd spend a bunch of money on them and feel very much like a noble martyr. Then that night one of them would be moping around the house, complaining about this or that. In righteous indignation, I'd really let him have it.

"How can you be that way after all Daddy did for you today? You certainly are an ungrateful child! I knock myself out to make things nice for you, and all I get is whine, whine, whine. You certainly seemed to be having a good time this afternoon. Do you have to be entertained every minute?"

Kids aren't dumb. They can figure that scene out. If they're going to get expressions of joy and pleasure thrown back in their faces (like when they're having fun at the circus), then they're not going to give out those good feelings. Why should they if they have to pay for them later? Then I grouse at my kids because they keep their feelings locked up inside. Their good feelings get thrown up to them when they're sad, and their bad feelings are rejected as an indication of how selfish and unappreciative they are. So they bury their feelings, and I sit and stew because my kids won't talk to me. Why couldn't I just have said, "I feel sort of frustrated when the things I do for you don't seem to keep you happy very long"?

Well, one reason is that I'm afraid to reveal that much about myself. I would have to accept personal responsibility for thinking and feeling in a way of which I'm not too proud. I'd like to think I'm the kind of father who understands that his kids don't have to pay him back for the nice things he does for them even though (and is this really so bad?) I do feast on their gratitude.

To let my kids or anyone else know my feelings puts me in a vulnerable position. Then they know how to get me. If they choose, they can tell me or show me that they don't like the kind of person I am. It makes me look, or at least I think it does, like a weakling. Aren't big, strong men who can make it "out in the world" supposed to be tougher than that? So I really don't want my hurt feelings to be the problem. I much prefer to come up with some rational explanation, coated with irrefutable logic, which makes it unquestionably clear, "That's the problem, and it's your fault!"

Another reason it's so difficult to express our feelings is that most people do such a poor job of receiving them. If you tell a friend how bad you are feeling, he or she tends to rush in with a bunch of sentimental comfort you don't want. What you want is understanding. I'll never forget talking to a woman who had recently gone through a painful divorce. She was really low. In the course of our conversation, she kept saying that all her friends were telling her how lucky she was to be rid of that no-good bum. But, as it turns out, there was something in her that still loved him. A part of her was deeply invested in him. She had borne his child. She wasn't able to cut all that out and say "Good riddance." She was willing to face the fact that they couldn't live together any more, but why wouldn't her friends let her feel sad and lonely because she had lost something that was important to her? Because it made them feel bad and because they didn't want her to feel bad. They refused to accept her real feelings.

If there is to be authentic communication, the way a feeling is received is just as important as the way it is expressed, and the receiving may be the more difficult task.

Not long ago, I was talking with a couple who had come to me to be married. I was stressing the importance of communicating their feelings to each other. In an effort to get them involved in the discussion, I said to the young man about his fiancée (who really was some kind of gorgeous gal), "I'll bet it makes you proud to take her to a party and let all the other guys see what a neat person wants to spend the rest of her life with you." By the way he responded, I could tell it was true.

As he talked, however, he got around to saying something else. Sometimes at those parties he got a little jealous of the attention the other fellows seemed to be getting from her. So he had both kinds of feelings, but when he started talking about the jealous feelings, his pretty bride-to-be couldn't stand it. "I don't know why you would ever feel that way. Don't you know you're the one I love?"

As soon as she said it, I flinched, and the next thing I did was to say to her, "I don't think that's fair." She was refusing to accept her fiancé's honest feeling. Did she feel guilty because maybe she enjoyed the attention of all those other men more than she wanted to admit, or did she just feel bad that her beloved had some insecurities? Probably both. Whatever the reasons, she crammed an honest feeling down his throat. If we hadn't gone on and looked at that some more (which we did), I suspect that fellow would have been reluctant to say so next time he was feeling something she didn't want to hear.

In effect, by her quick assurance of love, she was communicating to her fiancé, "You're stupid to feel that way. Any grown-up, right-thinking man should know that what goes on at parties is harmless. You must be some kind of inadequate person to have such a thought in your head. Shame on you!"

Now she didn't *know* she was saying that, and I feel sure she didn't *intend* to say that, but because she was unwilling to receive the honest expression of how he felt, that's what she communicated. We can all understand how much she didn't want him to feel that way, but if she wants to be married to *him*, she'd better hear him out. That *is* how he feels.

There are times, I suppose, when all of us feel it would be better to settle for a reasonably secure relationship that is a little bit phony than to risk a vital, alive relationship we can't ever get pinned down. That's a choice we have, but the choice for security, in this case at least, is a choice against being an authentic person and having a growing love relationship. If we are to be truly married to someone, then we will have to let him or her know who we are, and we have to be willing for him or her to say, "This is how it is with me."

I know a man who, when he gets home from work, usually goes straight to the kitchen where his wife is fixing supper. Sometimes he senses that something is wrong. She's not eager to talk about it; she knows how her bad feelings upset him. But he keeps insisting until it finally comes out. She's had a bad day. The kids have given her a lot of static. The washing machine broke down. She had all these things to do she didn't get done. How does he react? Well, her negative feelings scare him. So that's how he reacts.

He doesn't want his wife to be unhappy. When she is, it makes him feel as if he's not a good husband. He has this unrealistic image in his head of what a good husband is supposed to be. If he really is a good husband, he thinks, his wife will always be happy. So when his wife is unhappy, it makes him feel like a failure. This shattering of his self-image is frightening. Consequently, for all his purported concern, he isn't even listening to her.

Believing he is obliged to set things right (which really means trying to regain his own sense of being a good husband), this guy goes in and yells at the kids for making their mother unhappy, which doesn't make her any happier. Sometimes he tells her she shouldn't be unhappy. "Look at all the neat things I've done for you!" That makes her more unhappy. Sometimes he falls all over himself trying to do nice things for her, which makes her feel awkward and uncomfortable. Why can't he just accept the fact that as a person and as a mother of growing kids she's going to be unhappy sometimes? It's possible that her unhappiness doesn't have anything in the world to do with him. Why can't he see that? Because he doesn't want his fear to be the problem.

One thing more about the difficulty of receiving someone's real feelings: If we set ourselves to receive another person's authentic feelings, some of those feelings are bound to be angry and hostile. If we let people say only nice things to us, we will soon lose confidence in the authenticity of anything they say. It has been my experience that hostile feelings are never truly suppressed. They might not be mentioned, but they will come out one way or another, and any way they come out other than being talked about makes them almost impossible to handle.

The wildest example of this I've ever seen involved a meek-mannered little man and his domineering wife. They seemed to have a perfect marriage. It was obvious that she was the boss, but he didn't seem to mind. But something happened one day that blew the whole tranquil scene and sent them in for counseling.

The wife had gone upstairs to take a bath, but she couldn't get any hot water. She came downstairs to check. Her loving, acquiescent husband was standing at the kitchen sink with the hot-water tap going full blast. No wonder no hot water was getting upstairs. And he was grinning! That's what really got her. How could he take such fiendish delight in being mean to her? Didn't he love her any more?

It had to come out. One way or another, hostilities are going to come out—burned bacon, hard and silent stares across the bridge table, nasty comments about the in-laws. If we're able to talk them out, there is always some hope of finding a resolution, but if they aren't talked out, they will come out in some bizarre and destructive behavior that can't be handled.

We don't want feelings to be that important, but when it gets down to it, the other person's feelings are precisely what we want to know. I've had many couples describe their fights to me, for example, where he really was that night, who he was with, and what he was doing. Even if he is able to come up with plausible answers, the wife finds little satisfaction in them. What she really wants to know is "How do you feel about me? Do I still matter to you? Has anything changed?" That's what she wants to know but almost never asks.

Usually when I mention to a couple that it seems to me this is really what's at stake, they will readily agree. One terribly distraught wife even said, "Yes, that's really it. If I could be sure as to how he feels about me, I don't think I'd get upset if he stayed out all night."

In our personal relationships, feelings are finally what is at stake, but we don't want it that way. What often happens to us logical, analytical people is that we step out of the relationship, take a look at it, and say, "I see it all clearly now. It's your fault and here are the reasons." The difficulty is that when we step out of the relationship we don't see the relationship as it really is. We're not in it. For good or for ill, and usually both, we are part of whatever is going on in that relationship. Our feelings, our fears, and our hopes are a part of it—even if we don't want it to be that way.

6

THE PLACE TO BEGIN

If life is to be different and better for us, the most critical and necessary task is self-acceptance. Until we have been able to look at ourselves, at everything we are, be in touch with all our feelings, and say, "It's OK. I'm glad to be who I am," we will continue to be stuck with all the stifling despair of our fear that we do not matter.

Jess Lair's book, *I Ain't Much, Baby—But I'm All I've Got,* rambles across many chapters and many subjects. One little sentence, however, stuck away in the middle of his philosophizing and illustrations, says it clearly. "If you would give me five minutes for the whole book, that five minutes would be on acceptance of yourself—as you are." [1]

Self-acceptance is not easy. One of the most difficult parts is being able to look at *everything* in us that needs to be looked at. The chances are that we don't kid anyone

---

1. Jess Lair, *I Ain't Much, Baby—But I'm All I've Got* (Garden City, N.Y.: Doubleday, 1972), p. 53.

else more than we kid ourselves. Things about us that are inconsistent with the image we have of ourselves, we tend to rationalize away—which is just a sophisticated and sick form of rejection.

Until we have looked at everything, we cannot feel we have accepted ourselves. We have only accepted those parts of us that seem to merit acceptance. This, it seems to me, is the reason many Christians come across as rigid, stiff, and unloving. I am willing to give most of them credit for being serious about their faith, but they are unwilling to expose to God, or even to themselves, those parts of their life which do not measure up to their religious standards. Jesus himself got along better with tax collectors and prostitutes than with the rigorously religious. The people who were rejected and condemned by their society had nothing to hide. Because they were more willing to be who they were, they were able to experience the fullness of Jesus' acceptance.

Many of us who make a serious effort to be "good Christians" deny ourselves the warmth and joy of our faith because we are unwilling to admit our deep need to be loved and forgiven. In effect, we try to save ourselves by our good works, thus shutting the door on the grace and comfort of God.

I had an uncle who was a singularly good and proper man. He really was. His religion was rather stiff and hard, but there is no question in my mind that he was an ardent believer. A few years ago I ran into a man who had grown up as a kid in the town where my uncle lived. This man told me that as a teenager he had worked at the ice plant. Every Sunday, right after church, my uncle would drive into the ice plant and get a twenty-five-pound block of ice to make homemade ice cream. Every Sunday my uncle would say to the boy, now a man, who brought out the ice, "Charlie, don't you know you ought not work on the Sabbath?"

Finally, the ice-toting kid had enough. One particular

Sunday he swelled up his courage and said, "Mr. Ball, if people like you didn't come in here to buy ice on the Sabbath, I wouldn't have to work." The man told me that my uncle never came back again.

In an effort to get by on accepting only those portions of ourselves we regard as acceptable, we have to shrink our view of reality to manageable size. We have to pretend that the rest of the world and the rest of reality don't exist. We live in a fragile, self-constructed universe; we have to defend our self-made world from all who question its authenticity—and no one gives us more trouble than ourselves. We just can't seem to believe we are acceptable as we are.

However, acceptance is not the same as approbation or approval. If we look at ourselves honestly, we're going to find a lot of things that don't please us. To say "I did it and I'm glad" about those things is just another way of kidding ourselves. Acceptance simply means looking at everything and then saying, "Yes, that's me. For right now anyway, that's who I am."

The mystery is, that's the only way we can ever make real changes in our lives. As long as I kid myself about who I am and what's going on in my life, there's no way I can make authentic changes. In such a state, the only changes I make will be temporary and superficial. Alcoholics Anonymous won't even work with a person until he or she is willing to say, "I am a hopeless alcoholic." That's self-acceptance. It's not saying one is pleased to be that way; one's only desire is to change, but change cannot occur until the person is honest with himself or herself. *Change follows acceptance, not the other way around!*

There won't be any good and significant changes in our lives until from somewhere we find the courage to face and accept ourselves as we really are. I don't know of a more contemporary line in the whole Bible than the one describing the lawyer who came to Jesus and asked what he must do to have eternal life. Jesus asked what answer he would give, and the lawyer responded perfectly. "You shall love the Lord your God with all your heart, and with all your soul, and with all your strength, and with all your mind; and your neighbor as yourself" (Luke 10:27).

Jesus told the man he had it just right. If he followed those commandments, he would have all the fullness of life he ever wanted, but the man didn't want to get stuck with that. His own understanding of what was needed was too demanding. "But he, desiring to justify himself, said . . ." (Luke 10:29).

We live a good portion of our lives right there, "desiring to justify ourselves." Unimaginable amounts of energy and ingenuity go into that task. If nothing else, and there would be plenty else, our lives would be radically changed just by the time and effort we would have left over if we were ever to quit trying to justify ourselves. Can you even picture yourself going out into the world without trying to "snow" or impress anyone? It's hard even to imagine it. Justifying ourselves is a way of life with most of us.

One of the most important things I have discovered in trying to understand and accept myself is that I am a completely ambivalent person. Everything I feel and believe is matched by another feeling and belief in me that seems to contradict the first. If I cannot accept my ambivalence, I cannot accept myself.

For example, I really do believe in Jesus Christ. I am convinced that to depend on his love as the foundation for all living and to practice love in relationships is *the* way to life. However, something in me wishes that God didn't exist. He keeps getting in my way. As long as there is a God, the world is the way he made it rather than the way I want it to be. Something in me would like to forget about depending on love. I would prefer to depend only on me, on my brains, and on my shrewd maneuvering.

This same "something" thinks that to be loving is a burden and a bore. If things could be the way this something in me wants them, I would involve myself with other people only to the extent that they were useful and pleasing to me.

These feelings completely contradict my profession of faith in Jesus Christ, *but both sets of feelings really are a part of who I am*. If I try to kid myself, as I have done at times, into thinking that this second set of feelings doesn't really exist, I am refusing to face the reality of me. I'm fudging, and somewhere deep down inside I know it. As a result, my whole personality is filled with the air of phoniness, and this keeps me from feeling authentic even about the things I am willing to accept. If we aren't willing to be honest about the parts we don't like, neither can we be honest about the parts we do like. We either look at all of it, or we don't see any of it with authentic clarity.

Ambivalence runs through us from top to bottom. It isn't reserved for the religious realm. The persons I sincerely love the most are also the ones who vex, tire, and irritate me the most. If I'm not able to be honest about my irritation, neither will I be able to be honest about my love.

I want to get along with people and have them pleased with me, and I also want to be who I am, unique and independent from everyone else. I want to be a stable, respected member of the community, and I want to be a swinger. I see the benefits of being a hard and conscientious worker, and I have a certain jealousy of those who go along free and easy, just taking life as it comes.

In order to accept myself for who I really am, I must accept my ambivalence; and the things that matter the most are the things about which I am most ambivalent. I can deny the "dark" side of my personality, but I cannot get rid of it. If I deny it, I only push it underground where it continues to batter away at me, giving no relief.

It robs the joy from every honest pleasure and makes me strained and irritable in dealing with other people.

Obviously, I cannot act on both sides of my ambivalence at the same time; if I should try, I become hopelessly schizophrenic. Accepting both parts of me as really me is not the same as saying I'm going to act out everything I come up with in my ambivalence. Only as I recognize and accept both sides as a part of who I am do I put myself in a position to decide which set of feelings will lead to the life I want for myself.

Say, for example, that I am looking at both the side of me that desires to be loving and the side that wants to be completely selfish. They are both part of who I am, but as a person I have a choice to make. If I choose the loving way as the one I feel would be most contributory to the kind of life I want for myself and for the world, I am not denying that the selfish side exists. I'm simply saying, "This selfish part of me would make life miserable for me and for everyone else. I choose not to act on its urging."

That's completely different from telling myself, "All you feel is love and good will. Everything you do springs forth from a heart of pure devotion." Even if I end up doing the same thing, it's completely different. In the first case, I have faced myself and made a responsible choice. In the second, I'm playing a deceptive game. I come across to myself, and probably to others, as a phony.

Only when I have understood and accepted the ambivalence in myself am I able to accept ambivalence in others; if I cannot accept ambivalence in others, there is no way I can have an authentic relationship.

Everyone in the world is ambivalent. Take the parent-child relationship. Suppose one of my kids comes to me and says he hates me. It has happened. That's something I don't like to hear. If I don't understand about ambivalence, I get uptight and say, "Mercy me, what am I going to do? My child hates me. After all my effort and sacrifice for him, he hates me. I just can't let this happen. I must do something. What if he should go through the rest of his life hating his father? Mercy me!"

Understanding ambivalence makes that a completely different situation. I hear the kid say he hates me. I take him seriously. I know he is really angry about something. I can understand that. At times I have been angry with him. Anger is precisely what he is feeling at this moment, but I understand that isn't the only way he feels. I am able to give him the opportunity to be ambivalent, just as I have given it to myself.

If I fail to understand and accept his ambivalence, I focus everything on his anger. I may shame or scold or punish him for feeling that way. Whatever I do, I force him to get stuck on one leg of his ambivalence. He has to defend himself for feeling that way. By putting all my attention on anger as his only feeling, I deny him the opportunity to recognize that he has some feelings of love too. I force him to live on the narrow precipice of his hatred. I deny him the right to make a choice as to whether he is going to operate on the basis of his feelings of anger or his feelings of love.

For several years now, journalists and commentators in this country have talked a lot about the many divisions that exist among us. Everyone urges us to be more tolerant and understanding. I think that's starting at the wrong point. I cannot be more tolerant and loving toward others until I have learned to be tolerant and loving toward myself. As long as my sense of self-worth depends on maintaining a particular point of view or a particular style of life I regard as acceptable, anyone who disagrees must be proven wrong. If he should be right, I am wrong—more than wrong, I'm dead. My existence depends on the maintenance of my point of view.

But what if I, as a member of the establishment, were able to admit that there is within me some antiestablishment feelings? What if I had faced up to the fact that there are some things about straight lines and square corners that bug me? What if it were to come out that there are things about the military-industrial complex that make me uneasy? Isn't it possible that some people in the counterculture could then admit, "There are things about the free enterprise system and schedules and formal education and standards of morality that have meaning for me"?

I see no other place to begin. Self-acceptance is at the core of everything good we look for in our lives and in our society.

Probably a dozen years have gone by since I heard it, but I think of it often. A wise and learned man said to a group of us, "The most appealing thing about any person is his ability to live." That's one of those lines worth meditation. I've thought about the people who are most appealing to me, the ones I most enjoy being with. That's the kind of people they are. They have looked at themselves honestly, and they have looked at life realistically. Having looked, they've made a decision. They are *for* life and want to live.

They don't kid themselves about themselves nor about life. They know there are things about them that are not as they would like for them to be, and they know that life includes a lot of pain. But having looked at all of it, absolutely all of it, it comes out tipped on the side of hope and love. They decide that, being who they are, they want to live, that life is good and worth living. Their decision makes them positive and enthusiastic people, appealing.

Being the last child in a family has its drawbacks—hand-me-downs, having to stay at home when other kids go out, stuff like that—but it also has advantages. Mother and dad are usually a bit more mature and relaxed about being parents. As a last child, you have more people, the other kids in the family, to love you. Most "last kids" I have known have been open, enthusiastic people.

Nancy, the fourth and final kid in our family, is certainly that way. She really gives off signals that let you know she's glad to be alive. While she was still very young, one of my favorite things was to go to the grocery store with Nancy. It was an adventure. She didn't walk. She danced or skipped or ran everywhere. Every gaily colored box and every strange-shaped jar was a discovery. She was so glad to be alive that it made you glad also just being with her. I thought of the wise man's statement, "The most appealing thing about any person is his ability to live." It's true for all of us.

Self-acceptance is the beginning of everything. If we cannot be glad we are alive, nothing is going to seem good or hopeful. We cannot really enjoy other people for fear that when they find out how unacceptable we are they will reject us. God cannot be good, for if he were, he would not have made us and the world as unacceptable as we are. Self-acceptance opens us up to a new us, to new relationships with others, to a brand-new world.

A number of years ago I watched as two teenage sisters were playing with a small child. The two girls were close in age, both attractive, and both seemed to be trying to entertain the child in a similar way—running with him, holding him, and saying cute things to him.

I noticed that the child had a definite preference for one over the other. When the first girl chased after him, arms outstretched and saying loving things, the boy would run away, but when the other did the same thing, the child would go to her. What made the difference?

I knew both sisters, and they were different. The first girl really didn't like herself very much. She was pretty, made good grades, and had excellent manners; but she had little confidence that she was someone others would like. As a consequence, when she held the child, he experienced her "taking" love from him more than "giving" it. She wanted assurance of her worth more than she wanted to assure the child of her love. The child didn't like that. He felt used. He instinctively drew away from a person who wanted to suck life out of him for herself.

The other girl, by any external standards of measurement, didn't have any more going for her than her sister did, but she was different. She seemed to believe that she was an "OK person." Being a teenager, she probably hadn't probed through all this to any great depth; yet, in her own way, she had decided she was OK. She accepted herself as someone worth knowing. That's how she came across. Because she was able to enjoy herself, the child was able to enjoy her also.

That's how it works. Self-acceptance is the beginning of everything.

7

BEING DIFFERENT ISN'T BAD

One of my favorite theories has no scholarly or statistical evidence to back it up. Nevertheless, I believe that what we think of another person is 80 percent us and only 20 percent them. I'm suggesting that only about one-fifth of who that other person is gets through to us, which leaves four-fifths of what we think of him or her to be made up out of our own hopes, fears, and neuroses.

Though I have no academic authorities to substantiate my theory, I can tell you what got it started. A close friend told me one day, "Bob, you make my wife very nervous. Every time she's around you, she gets the feeling you're psychoanalyzing her."

"That's interesting, Jack," I replied, "because I have the feeling your wife doesn't like me. So every time I'm around her, I make an effort to withdraw to the sidelines, to be very quiet and unobtrusive. I don't want to give her any more reasons for not liking me than she already has."

The longer I have thought about this and the more

people I talk to about it, the more convinced I am that this is a picture of what goes on between people all the time. Because of my fear that this woman didn't like me, I treated her as if she didn't. How I saw her had a lot more to do with me than with her. Because of how I was, I decided how she was. She did the same. Because my manner made her uncomfortable, she decided I was analyzing and judging her. What she thought of me had a lot more to do with how she felt about herself than it did with how I was. I think this happens all the time.

We would like to have friends. We would like for people to like us. I just can't buy the idea some people put out that "I don't care one whit what other people think of me." We all need to know we matter, and though our sense of mattering needs to be internalized, I don't think we can invent it. We experience ourselves as persons of worth when some other person cares about us.

We would like to have friends, but having and keeping friends is one of the most difficult jobs in the world. We just can't seem to help being fearful of how other people are going to react to us and receive us. No matter how much we may understand it intellectually, when we get in an emotional crisis, it is hard to remember that other person is yearning for acceptance just as much as we are.

My 80 percent–20 percent theory has been helpful in this connection. When I get the feeling a person is rejecting me, I remember it's probably 80 percent my rejection of myself. That doesn't solve the problem, but it does allow me to work on it at a more appropriate point. Sometimes it keeps me from getting angry and defensive, and the relationship is spared a lot of gook that can totally bury it.

As I tried to spell out in the preceding chapter, my acceptance of myself allows me to accept other people. The things about other people that annoy, frighten, and anger me the most are usually the things I have not come to terms with in myself. I discovered, for example, in a church that I served as pastor, that in my sermons I would frequently drop a sarcastic line about the "country club people." A number of people in the congregation were members of fashionable country clubs. At first glance, it might appear that I was very courageous in being willing to say what I thought about the "country club people" to their faces. On second thought, it wasn't quite face-to-face. I had a black robe and a pulpit between me and them. I'm sure I was not equally as courageous in a one-to-one situation.

On third thought, I began to realize that belonging to a country club represented, symbolically, to me a high level of attainment, one that had some fascination for me but to which I was never likely to attain. Once I faced this desire to prove myself successful by my social status, I found I was able to say what needed to be said to and about the "country club people" more authentically. Until I had faced it, I was really taking unfair potshots to satisfy my repressed frustration.

When I feel about or tell someone, in whatever words, "You're no damn good," I'm probably saying, "You make me feel like I'm no damn good."

One of the most horrible three hours of my life was riding back from out of town with a guy who, for reasons not completely clear to me, didn't like me. The trip had no sooner started than he took in after me. He let me know in no uncertain terms that I was a real loser, a bad guy, a drag on society. Fortunately, I was driving, and I drove fast. If that trip had lasted another five minutes, I think I would have been destroyed. I was pretty badly shaken as it was.

Years later, looking back on the experience, I still don't know just what it was that made it necessary for that guy to get me, but I'm sure he did. That has to be his problem. I am not saying there are no reasons for anyone to find fault with me, but when a person needs to destroy me, he has some frightened and negative thoughts about himself.

I need to have a place to stand in the world, a place where I can feel reasonably safe and worthwhile. If someone tries to take my place away from me, I'm either going to have to fight him or capitulate and die—unless my place is built on such an authentic foundation that he cannot take it from me.

Recognizing my need for a place to stand, I need to recognize also that every other person has exactly the same need. If I come on in such a way that I threaten another person's place to stand, he or she is going to fight me. If I attack or belittle a person's sense of self-worth, nothing constructive can happen for either of us.

Several years ago we made a rule in our family: Everyone is an expert in his or her own feelings. No matter how smart or insightful I may become, there is no way I can know better than you do what you're feeling. One night not too long after the rule was made, my son Randy, who was about ten at the time, got up from the dinner table, saying, "I hate school, and my teacher is the worst in the whole world."

I was shrewd enough to figure out what was going on. Randy's favorite TV show was about to come on, but he had a bunch of homework. With the benefit of my great insight, I began to explain: "Randy, you don't hate school. I know you want to watch television and . . ."

Randy cut me off. "Hey, dad. I thought we agreed that everyone in this family is an expert in his own feelings."

What could I say? "You're right. Would you tell me once more what your feelings are?"

"I hate school, and my teacher is the worst teacher in the world."

"Okay, I hear you. I understand that you hate school and don't like your teacher. I'm sorry that you feel that way, but I understand that you do."

With that, Randy picked up his books, went upstairs, and began to study. It was OK. He still didn't get to watch television, but that wasn't the most important issue. He had been given the right to have his place to stand. It was his, and no one was taking it away from him. That's important. Isn't that something like what it means to respect someone as you respect yourself?

When we can allow people the right to their feelings, let them feel safe about expressing them, never make them feel sorry they told us how it is with them, we have done much to enhance their sense of self-worth. When a person isn't free to be expert in his or her own feelings, our relationship is inauthentic and destructive.

"I Feel" communications are the key to any relationship, but being "brutally frank" is not the same as making "I Feel" statements. Just to tear into another person and tell him or her how bad you think he or she is, is not the deepest thing you are feeling. Down beneath all that anxiety is some fear. If you're really going to "tell it like it is," you're going to have to talk about your fears.

One of the most exciting things we discover when we do this is that both of us are looking for the same thing, for the assurance that we matter. When I understand that what you want is what I want, I feel closer to you. No longer do I see you as a threat to my sense of worth; rather, I am able to live with you as a fellow traveler. When we have learned to accept ourselves and one another, we often discover that we find our joy in helping another find what he or she needs.

If we could only learn to accept ourselves and one another, perhaps much of our bitter warfare would be over —within ourselves, in our families, in the world.

The following story is a practical example of the difference it makes when a person is able to accept himself or herself and others. The story is true, but the names are changed to protect those whose innocence got them into a mess.

Bill and Mary looked forward with keen anticipation to the arrival of their first child. Because of his background and personality, Bill tended to be authoritarian. Mary was the other way. If it were possible to rate it on a scale, Bill went into his first experience of parenthood about five notches to the authoritarian side of zero, and Mary about five notches toward permissiveness. Though they had never even thought about it in those terms, each assumed that his or her position was the correct spot—dead zero.

As the months with the new baby went by, Bill became more and more vexed at how lenient Mary was (remember that Mary was ten notches away from Bill's position). So Bill cranked himself out about five more notches to compensate for Mary's laxity. As Mary saw Bill becoming more and more of a tyrant, she felt compelled to become more and more permissive, at this point about five notches more. As the first child got older and then a second child came, Bill and Mary both got farther and farther away from the center—and from each other.

The situation finally became so extreme that they had to talk about what was happening. Bill was so far out that almost everything he had to say to the kids was condemning and critical. Mary had become so permissive that the kids just ran over her. Neither liked where he or she was, but each was afraid to "give in" (which is what going back the other way seemed like). Bill felt that since Mary was so permissive, the whole family situation would become absolute anarchy if he relented at all. Mary was afraid to get tough. Add that to what Bill was doing and their home would be like a concentration camp. So they were stuck; neither wanted to be where he or she was and neither knew how to get out of the assumed position.

With the help of a counselor, Bill and Mary were able to see what had happened. They heard the counselor say that having one parent who is five notches to the authoritarian side of center and one five notches in the direction of permissiveness is the best possible arrangement for rearing a child. It allows the child to get used to dealing with authoritarian types and permissive types in a context of love. The child needs to know how to deal with both; he or she is going to run into a lot of them "out in the world." The counselor went so far as to say that a child reared by two "perfectly adjusted" parents would probably have a rough time outside the home, since there aren't a great many "perfectly adjusted" people.

So Bill and Mary made a decision. Bill would accept himself as being five notches from zero in the direction of authoritarianism, which was much more comfortable for him than where he had gotten himself—something like fifty notches away; Mary agreed that she would accept Bill as being that way, even to the extent of appreciating that his natural posture added something important to the family's life. Mary would accept herself in the position of five notches away from center in being permissive, and Bill, with his new insight in the situation, said he thought he could even learn to be glad Mary was that way.

We don't have to be like everybody else, and we don't even have to conform to some psychological "norm" in order to be good, constructive persons. Neither do we have to insist that everybody else be like us to be contributing members of society. God made each of us unique with different gifts and abilities to share. A marriage, a family, a church, a community, a country, a world are richer and fuller when everyone is allowed to express his or her uniqueness, allowed to contribute what he or she has. When that uniqueness is denied, everyone gets flattened into the same dull nothingness, or, as in the case of Bill and Mary, a royal battle ensues which drives everyone to an extreme where they aren't their real selves at all.

People are different. Sometimes that will vex us, even cause us pain, but being different isn't bad. As a matter of fact, it has the potential of being very, very good. Learning to appreciate and accept ourselves allows us to begin to do the same for others; the end result is a stronger, more creative society.

8

ASK FOR WHAT YOU WANT

How do we change over to this new way of communicating? How do we set the stage for some "I Feel" conversations? We need a new contract.

We refer sometimes to the "marriage contract," but few people take that seriously. To speak of marriage as a contract sounds so unromantic! Well, whether we like it or not, marriage is a contract. Spoken or unspoken, each of us goes into marriage with some expectations of what we're going to do and what we're going to get out of the relationship. By any other name, that's still a contract, and the expectations are its clauses.

I mentioned earlier how our "disappointed expectations" can lead to turmoil in marriage. That's an example of the problems that arise when the contract is not understood. Often, what one person wants very much out of the marriage is a complete mystery to the other. The first person thinks the second knows what is wanted but just won't give it. As a result, the first feels cheated and short-changed because he or she is not getting needs met, but he or she never took the time to say directly, "This is something I would like to have."

Someone, I think it was Fritz Perls, said, "People change, but they forget to tell each other." That's important to understand. Maybe two people have gone with each other long enough before they get married to have a fair idea of what the other person wants. They understand and they are willing to live with that contract. But people don't stay the same. As the years go by, there are new associations, new job responsibilities, new demands (like children) in the home, new books which get read, and new friends. All these contribute to the creation of a new set of needs.

This old boy is going along thinking he's doing such a great job of being a husband. Then one day to his utter surprise and chagrin, his wife begins to tell him how terribly unhappy she is. He's dumbfounded. He thought he was performing admirably. Maybe he was, but it was under the terms of the old contract. It never occurred to him that things might change, and apparently it never occurred to his wife that she should tell him when they do.

I've about decided that every marriage contract ought to be reexamined and renegotiated every six months. As fast as things are changing in the world around us, it might need to be more often than that. If people are going to live in a personal relationship with each other, they had better be willing to take the time to listen and find out "how it is" with the other person.

Renegotiating a contract isn't always fun, but it doesn't need to be as painful as solitary confinement. Most of us tend to feel secure when things stay just as they have always been. Change is frightening. It forces us to work out who we are and where we are all over again.

Change is a reality that needs to be faced. There has always been change, but never at the rate at which we are being subjected to it today. We need to understand why change is such a threat to us—and it *is!*

For example, if a man had been living in the same house with the same furniture arrangement for twenty years, he could come home late at night and, without the help of a light, find his way wherever he wanted to go. But suppose that while he was gone one day somebody came in and rearranged all the furniture. So the man comes home, all innocent and unaware. First thing he knows, he's fallen over a chair he didn't know was there. In falling, he knocks over a table and pulls an heirloom lamp down on top of him. He lies there dazed. His shin hurts where he hit the chair. That precious lamp he has protected so carefully for years is smashed to pieces, and his hands are bleeding from the broken debris. But the most frightening thing of all is that he doesn't know what has happened! *He no longer knows where he stands in relation to what is!*

That's what change does to us. As long as we know who loves us and who hates us, what works and what doesn't, we can set ourselves to the tasks of getting what we want and dealing with the problems. But when we aren't familiar with the reality around us, we don't know what to do. That's a frightening, helpless feeling, and a lot of people experience it today. Those who sing songs about how great everything was back in the "olden days" aren't going to change their tune by having it pointed out to them that there were a lot of things in the "olden days" they didn't like at all. That's not the point. The point is that they thought they knew how things were back then, and, knowing, they felt able to deal with them. The terrifying thing about the new is that it is new, and we don't know where we stand in relation to it.

It's possible that the man in the rearranged house might find that he really likes the new arrangement better. But that won't happen until somehow he's been able to get off the floor, find some medicine for his hurts, and starts making an effort to understand the new arrangement. As long as he stays there on the floor, screaming about his hurts and cursing whoever so thoughtlessly changed things without asking him, life is going to be miserable and unproductive.

I'm not suggesting that change for the sake of change is good. Things aren't necessarily better just because they are different, and a lot of things out of the past are well worth preserving—things that have proven deeply satisfying and of life-giving benefit to people over a long period of time. But change is a reality we can't stop, no more than the woman could stop the flood by trying to sweep the water out of her house with a broom. Unless we think we have arrived at such perfection within ourselves and within the world that no more improvement is needed, some changes are necessary.

What we most need to change is our attitude about change. Change is always *experienced* as loss. Any change takes from us something that was a part of our lives, something we knew and understood well enough to know where we stood in relation to it. We need to recognize that change is part of life. Change is going to happen. Some changes we can't do anything about; some, we can. Understanding this, we will not be so likely to resist all change, and neither will we be so apt to rush out and embrace all change as if "anything is better than what I've got now."

Having at least some idea of what life is all about—loving and respecting God and other people and ourselves—we can dare to experiment with some new possibilities that show hope for accomplishing those ends. The ones that don't work we can throw away. We will have at least learned in the experience. The changes that do foster new understanding and enhance the dignity of being human are a real gain. We have done some growing, and the world is a better place in which to live.

Mabel gets involved in a church discussion group on

interpersonal relationships and goes home all fired up about communicating on a feeling basis. Her husband is threatened. That was never in their contract. What do they think they're doing down there at the church, messing up his happy home? He and Mabel got along fine for years. They don't need any of this liberal, fuzzy-headed thinking to ruin their happy home. But Mabel has a new vision. She has discovered some new possibilities and some new needs. She wants a new contract.

If the husband happens to be satisfied with the old contract, if it is allowing him the rewards and freedoms he wants, he's not likely to be favorably inclined toward drawing up a new one which requires something different of him. His only choice, however, is to go on kidding himself, to play "God Almighty," saying, "I know what is good for my wife in spite of what she says." He might be tough enough to enforce a contract like that, but it will not be a shared life between two persons.

If there is to be a new and personal relationship, there must be a new contract. There must be a willingness to say, and to allow the other person to say, "This is how it is with me, and this is what I feel I need out of our marriage." After you get that out, and I think it is good to write these things down, then you start negotiating. When you get to the tough parts, there may have to be some compromising, some giving here for the sake of something else over there. That's OK. Nobody knows beforehand just how it will work out. If some clause in the contract or some compromise doesn't work, then a week later you go back to the bargaining table to try something else. Painful it may be, but it is also exciting, alive, and real. And what's more, in the process you *are* communicating.

I tell all the couples I marry that when you condense the meaning of all words in the marriage ceremony, this contract emerges: I promise that I will be *for* you. That, it seems to me, is the basic, essential, and nothing-at-all-without contract in the marriage relationship.

To promise to be *for* a person does not mean you are going to feel good about him or her all the time. To assume that you will, and many do seem to assume that, is to head for giant disillusionment. If you have the idea that your marriage depends upon the two of you always feeling good about each other, there will be lots of days when you don't have much of a marriage.

You can commit yourself to be *for* a person, and act in ways that are *for* him or her, even when you don't feel good about that person. After all my talk about being authentic, I'm not now asking you to start faking it. On the contrary, to be *for* a person simply means that you will not act in ways that are *against* him. It means that when you get angry you will say so and, insofar as you are able, tell why—instead of burning the bacon or saying you have a headache for the tenth straight night or making sarcastic little comments about how he or she doesn't seem to be moving ahead very fast at the office.

To be *for* a person means that who he or she is and what he or she wants is important to you. It doesn't mean that you will always agree or always be pleased with that person. It means committing yourself to do what you can to respect him or her as a person. To be *for* a person means you will not act in ways that are *against* him or her.

There will be times when we do act in ways that are *against* the person we have committed ourselves to be *for*. Sometimes it happens deliberately; more often, thoughtlessly. Either way, it is a hurt. It is breaking the contract. When it happens, we need to say, "I'm sorry."

A line from a popular novel that became a movie and later became the title of a song from that movie said, "Love means never having to say you're sorry." I don't believe that, but I think I understand why that notion would arise. Often it's extremely vexing for someone to say "I'm sorry." You may feel like a beast for not warming up to the apology (another song of older vintage said, "What can I say, dear, after I've said, 'I'm sorry'?"), but sometimes it rankles nonetheless. One reason for this, I think, is that many apologies don't really change anything. It's like the other person is saying he or she is miserable because we're having a squabble. Well you are too, but it didn't change the situation for that person to say "I'm sorry we're both so unhappy."

But with a new understanding of the contract, saying "I'm sorry" is different. It means something specific, and it changes things. It means "I know I failed our contract, and this is where I did it. The way in which I acted was not *for* you. I'm sorry. I really do want to be *for* you, and I commit myself again to that contract. I cannot promise never to fail you again, but I do want you to know that my commitment is to be *for* you."

That, I think, is how relationships grow. Our growth as persons and in relationships does not take place on a straight line, always shooting upward. We go along for a while without much of anything happening. Then some crisis comes along and the bottom drops out. We're miserable, and that's when we learn. We take a new look at ourselves, at the other person, at what is going on in our relationship. Then, fortified with new insights and making a new commitment, we shoot forward.

After a while it doesn't completely throw us when crises come along. That doesn't mean that we should look forward to them; they're miserable to go through. But over a period of time we discover that we can come out of crises, and more than just come out. The new things that happen in the midst of the crisis push us to greater maturity. So even if we can't look forward to the crises, we can learn not to be afraid of them. We can even go into them with hopeful anticipation. "I'm going to come out of this a more mature human being than I am now."

For a lot of reasons, our fear of rejection and the conditioning of our culture are among them, one of the most difficult tasks is to ask for what we want. We come at it in oblique, manipulating ways. For example, the family is out driving, and you pass an ice cream store. One of the kids says, "Hey, Dad, have you got any money?" Why couldn't he just say "I surely would like to have an ice cream cone"? Because he has learned from living with us that people don't come on that straight. Many questions are really statements in disguise; so the question is dishonest.

When a child is on the way out the door to school and mother says, "Aren't you going to wear your coat today?" what she really means is "It's rainy and cold, and I want you to wear your coat." But that isn't what she said. A husband comes home from work after a hard, tiring day. His wife says, "Would you like to go to a movie tonight?" He may say, "No, not really. I'm pretty tired. But I'll go if you want to. Do you?" And his wife will probably reply, "Oh, no, I just thought you might like to go." Then she may very well pout and be cold all evening because he wouldn't take her to the movies, but she never did ask for what she wanted.

Some people with whom I've talked about this tell me, "But that takes all the romance out of it. It's no fun being loved if you have to ask for it." Of course, it's exciting to be surprised, but it's dishonest to expect something from someone without saying so. If you want that kind of a relationship, you'd better try to marry a mind reader. Expecting but not asking puts a lot of pressure on the other person. He or she has to be very attentive and careful to pick up the signals. The only thing that pouting, being silent, or yelling is that he or she hasn't yet figured out what it is we want.

Actually there's less rejection experienced in asking for what you want than in putting out a dishonest question. If a man asks his wife, "Do you want to make love tonight?" and she answers, "Well, I'm awfully tired, but we can if you want to," he's likely to say, "Oh, go to sleep." Then he'll roll over feeling hostile, hurt, and rejected, and she'll lie there feeling guilty, unappreciated, and angry. The dishonest question that was really a statement set up a situation in which both ended up feeling rejected.

If the husband had said, "I'm feeling romantic and would like to make love," he would have been coming on straight. Even if his wife had answered, "I really feel so tired that I don't think I have much to share tonight," that could have been handled. The husband might well feel some disappointment, but he wouldn't need to feel rejected. He had been straight with himself and with his wife, and she had been straight with him. We won't always get what we want when we ask for it, not from God or from other people, but asking for what we want is the only way to have an honest, open relationship.

Within that kind of relationship, spontaneous, exciting things are more likely to happen. If we go around feeling hostile and sorry for ourselves because that other person hasn't done for us what we think he should, that other person will feel our disappointment and unhappiness. He won't be likely to spend much time thinking of fun things to do to show how much he enjoys us and the relationship. But when the relationship is open and honest, when both parties feel affirmed and authentic, it becomes a joy to think of happy surprises the other will enjoy.

Jesus said, "Ask, and it will be given you; seek, and you will find; knock, and it will be opened to you" (Matt. 7:7). And it all begins with *ask*.

9

THE GIANT COMMUNICATOR

This is a book on communication, and I regard sex as *the* most sensitive and expressive means of communication that exists between two human beings. In fact, as I see it, that's what sex is—a means of communication. Understanding sex in that way has been exceedingly helpful to me, both in trying to understand my own sexuality and in talking with others about theirs.

Centuries ago, Socrates began the philosophical search with the admonition, "Know thyself." That quest, the search for personal identity, is still running at high tide. But hardly any material I have read about knowing one's self deals very seriously with the most obvious fact about us: All of us are either male or female, and how we feel about that fact of who we are is crucial in our life-experience.

Early in life, even before we are consciously aware of it, we begin to pick up signals about our sexuality. Psychological researchers say that it registers with an infant as to whether or not his or her diaper is changed just by mother or also by father. Each family has norms about whether members of the family run around the house half-clad or whether one is always expected to wear a robe. The reaction a child gets from parents when his exploring hands find his genitals makes an impression. We begin to develop a consciousness as to how we feel about ourselves as sexual beings.

I remember my first "date" clearly. I was thirteen. I put on my "Ike jacket" (for you youngsters, they were popular during World War II), billowed a while silk scarf at the neck like an ace pilot, and knocked at her front door. We walked the seven or eight blocks to the picture show, bought a box of popcorn, and sat down.

I remember vividly, as if it was yesterday, how fervently I wanted to hold her hand. I spent the entire movie with my arms resting casually (?) on the divider armrest between us. Out of the corner of my eye I could see her hand lying there so sweet and inviting, just about eight inches below where mine was poised with its teenage passion. I thoughtfully considered all the ways my hand might travel that short but terrifying distance. I could let my arm fall off the divider, as if by accident, and there I would be. Or I could boldly, but tenderly, reach down and take hold of her inviting fingers. I considered all the possibilities, but I followed through on none of them.

What was the problem? Since I was male and she was female, to hold her hand would have been a sexual expression, and I was uncertain as to my sexual acceptability. I was aware that she liked me enough to go to a movie with me, but maybe that was just because she liked Roy Rogers and popcorn. The big question in my mind (though, at the time, I was not aware that this was the question) was, What do you think of me as a male? Is my maleness acceptable to you?

I never found out. My arm stayed in its poised position

through the whole movie, but it never struck. The fear of rejection was too intense. When the movie was over we left, walked those seven or eight blocks back to her house, and said good night. A month or so later we repeated the same procedure all over again with the same result. It was too frustrating. I gave up. I never called her again.

A couple of months later at our church's Christmas party, this girl came up to me, handed me a note, and walked away. I no longer have the note, but I remember exactly what it said. "Dear Bob, I don't blame you for not liking me now, but I can't help how I felt about you for those two months." I still haven't figured out what the first part meant, but the second I understand quite clearly. *She wanted her hand to be held just as much as I wanted to hold it.* She was just as eager for assurance that she was an acceptable, desirable female as I was yearning to be assured of the acceptability of my maleness. But neither of us got what we wanted because I was afraid.

And so it goes. Our feelings about ourselves as sexual beings continue to build. The girl who won't let you kiss her good night, or the boy who doesn't try. The scary (and totally erroneous) stories you hear about masturbation, and the reports of the boys in the locker room about their sexual conquests. Girlie magazines and X-rated movies. Whether or not people laugh at your dirty stories, and the acne on your face. All these and a thousand other experiences influence our sense of sexual acceptability. By the time newlyweds crawl into bed for their "first night," dozens of other people are in that bed with them: a procession of people have contributed to how they feel about themselves as sexual beings.

The big question on that night is, How'd I do? Do I turn you on? Do you think I'm a great lover? It's all a pivotal part of the big question: Is it true, as I fear it is, that I don't matter, or do you find me very special? This is why it seems to me that sex is the most sensitive and expressive means of communication between two human beings. Sex is at the heart of our anxiety as to whether or not we matter.

I have talked to highly successful businessmen, the kind who have three phones on their desks and staff people running in every direction, who have serious questions about their worth because they can't seem to turn their wives on at night. What happens at the office is important to their self-image, but, in a strange sort of way, it all seems to be happening outside them. The crucial test of their worth comes when they take off their clothes, when there is no title engraved on the door and no double-knit suit to make them look impressive. Here I am, just as I am. What do you think of *me*?

It's significant, you see, that the sex act is done with our clothes off. We are actually, as well as symbolically, naked and vulnerable. I have nothing to protect me or promote me. Now we're really down to it. What do you think of the naked me? Are you going to laugh at me, be disappointed in me, reject me? I am defenseless before you. What you think of me now makes a lot of difference in how I'm going to feel about myself.

But if it should happen that you like me, that you find me exciting and desirable, oh, brother! That would fill my cup of confidence to overflowing. You like me! You are glad I am who I am! You let me know that I matter! Sex is great!

The satisfaction we find in our sexual relationships depends to a large extent on how we feel about ourselves. To the extent that I am scared, uncertain, and have negative feelings about myself, I will focus on proving that none of these things are true, and I will hardly be aware of you at all—except in terms of how you are responding to me. You may very well get the feeling you are being "used," for, as a matter of fact, you are—used to prove what I can't believe about myself.

But to whatever degree I genuinely like me, regard

myself as someone worth knowing, I will be released to share my pleasure in being alive with you. When I am no longer hung-up with proving something about myself, I am free to express to you how much I enjoy you. That's why honeymoons are frequently a source of "disappointed expectations." The anxious questions both persons are asking about themselves prevent their being able to communicate anything deeply satisfying to each other. It takes time. It gets better. A good friend of mine who has been married over thirty years tells me sex has never been better for him than it is today. I find that encouraging.

And it's all a process of communication. Suppose, for example, it's your first week on a new job with a big company. The boss calls you into the office for a "get acquainted" session. You discuss everything from company policies to the possibilities of global war. How relaxed and easy are you going to feel in letting him or her know who you really are? Not very. You want to make a good impression. You want the boss to like you and to be impressed with how sharp you are. I suspect you would experience a good bit of self-consciousness and awkwardness.

Now let's say you have been with the company for ten years. You have done well. It is obvious that they are pleased with your work. You have gotten promotions and increases in pay. You are aware that you are respected and important to the company. Now you're having another conversation with the big boss. It's different, isn't it? You feel considerably more confident in letting him or her know how you feel about whatever you're discussing. The self-consciousness and awkwardness are gone. It's fun, letting the other person know who you are and finding out how it really is with him or her. The difference is that now you know that you matter. You aren't trying to prove yourself. The two of you can communicate more authentically.

That's how it is in sexual relationships. When, over a period of time, we find ourselves accepted, desired, and appreciated, we can relax. We are more willing to let who we are be known and to allow the other person to tell us how it is with him or her. The dozens of anxious questions that have been hovering over the bed like a wet blanket are gone. We are free to engage in an authentic "I Feel" relationship, and it's great.

Sex seems to be the most expressive way available for saying, "You matter to me," *and that is the one thing we want most of all to hear.*

If sex is so great, why does it cause us so many problems? The very thing that makes it great also makes it potentially destructive. If sex has the capacity to give us deep confidence in our self-worth, it also has the potential to destroy it. If you don't like the naked "me," the most vulnerable revelation of who I am, then I'm going to be hostile and defensive toward you. I'm not going to let you get too close to me, for I fear you would destroy me. I'm going to turn away from you and seek elsewhere the assurance I need so desperately—the assurance that I indeed matter.

I have found it helpful in examining "sex problems" to ask, Where has the communication broken down? I ask the people involved to look at what they have to say to each other, that is, at how they really feel about themselves and the other person. Whatever they happen to be feeling, that's what gets communicated through their sexual relationship.

If there is resentment, that comes through. If there is weak-kneed fear, it is felt. If there is a desperate, clinging, suffocating yearning for assurance, the other person feels buried beneath all those needs. The solution to these problems, it seems to me, is not to be found in better sex techniques but in looking at and working on how we feel about ourselves and what we have to say to each other.

As I talk to kids about their sexual fears and frustrations, I frequently discover that their problems arise from trying to say more through sex than they actually have to say. The problem, therefore, is inauthentic communication. This guy, let's say, wants so much to be assured that he is loved, that this chick thinks he's the greatest thing in the world, that she is so knocked in the head with him that there's no way she could hold anything back from him. So he tries to force, through sexual expression, a relationship between them which does not, in fact, exist. It may or may not seem deliriously wonderful at the moment, but that night when he gets home, he feels punk. He knows he was living out a lie.

He really doesn't trust her all that much. He really isn't willing to let her know his naked self. He is not, in truth, so completely committed to her that he is willing to accept her complete trust of him. What they seemed to be saying to each other through their sexual expressions isn't the truth. A person has to begin playing some destructive games with himself or herself to be convinced that he or she enjoys living out a lie.

The stories of those who use sex to say more than they do, in fact, have to say to each other make headlines. I am convinced, however, that there are just as many problems on the other side, people who have something authentic to say to each other, things that can only be expressed through sex, which never get said.

A beautiful, intelligent, sensitive high-school senior came to see me one day. We had visited before, so there was already a comfortable friendship between us. Our conversation began to focus on the fact that she had no boyfriends. She had lots of boy "friends," guys who liked to come around the house, engage her in long conversations, and eat her mother's cookies, but no one who really seemed to notice that she was a girl.

The further we got into it, the more she talked about one particular guy. He came to her house often. He liked to look at her drawings and read her poetry, but he never asked her for a date. She would like for him to do just that. She wanted to be more than a "sister" to him. She wanted to be appreciated as a woman, but what could she do?

I made a suggestion. "Next time he comes over, while he's sitting there on the divan looking at your scrapbook, go over and sit beside him. After a little while, try putting your hand up on the back of his neck. I'll bet that guy will jump right out of his skin."

Hardly the advice you would expect a pastor to give a teenager? Perhaps. But I kept remembering the little girl whose hand I wanted to hold and who wanted her hand held. I felt that this girl I was talking to had something authentic she wanted to say to her friend, but how do you put it into words? How do you say "I really do like you. I enjoy being with you. It pleases me that you are a boy, and you make me glad to be a girl"? It's hard to "say" it; it needs to be shown! So that's why I told her what I did. I cannot give you a factual report on the outcome, but the next Sunday morning she gave me an extra big smile when she walked out after the worship service.

"The most appealing thing about any person is his ability to live." When you run into someone who has looked at life as it really is, not hiding his or her eyes from anything, and has decided that he or she really is glad to be alive, that's someone you want to be with. And that, somehow, is how I see sex at its very best: one person saying to another in the most expressive way possible, "I'm so delighted to be alive, to be who I am, and to be sharing this wonderful life God has given me with you. You are special to me."

10

"I FEEL" PRAYERS

Several years ago the "God is dead" movement burst into bloom. It didn't last long, but for a short time it was the rage, even made the cover of *Time* magazine. The phrase originated with Nietzsche in the last century, but it took on many different meanings in the 1960s.

A great many church people were offended at the impudent impiety, which caused them to miss what was, for me, one of the most significant parts of the movement. For some writers, the point was that to live in a formal, noninvolved intellectual faith in God was the same as treating him as if he were dead. It's true. If you walked around in your house day after day doing things, speaking to people, letting them know how you feel and all you got in return was an occasional "Sure, fine, that's great," but no one ever took you or your feelings seriously, wouldn't you begin to think they were treating you as if you were dead?

Isn't that how many of us treat God a good bit of the

time? When we talk to him, if we do at all, isn't it usually something rather formal and proper without much personal meaning or feeling? How serious are we about letting him and his truth become functioning parts of who we are?

Now it isn't my purpose to make anyone feel guilty about the quantity or quality of his or her prayer life. I think there is already enough guilt about prayer abroad in the land. In fact, to me, that's one of the biggest mistakes the churches make, coming at people in such a way as to make them feel guilty. That isn't to say we aren't guilty. It's just that most people already have more guilt than they can handle anyway. They don't need any more. Often the church uses guilt as a means of gaining converts, enlisting Sunday school teachers, and raising money for the budget. That may be an effective way to get the job done, at least temporarily, but I'm not at all sure it's Christian.

I'd like to come at prayer from a different direction. If we were to agree that life is about relationships (and we would have a good deal of support from the behavioral scientists to back up that conviction) and if we were to agree that communication is the most important means by which relationship is established and is maintained and grows, then the communication we share with God would have to be one of the most important experiences in our lives.

If we do not participate in a communicative relationship with God, we're missing the opportunity for direct contact with the source of life itself. When it seems that God is dead, it may be that we are the dead ones, no longer allowing ourselves to be involved with life's deepest reality. The French philosopher, Voltaire, is reported to have said about God, "We salute, but we do not speak." That sort of mechanical honoring of God is not likely to do any more for our personal relationship with him than it does in getting to know our spouses.

Without prayer, deeply personal and authentic prayer, life becomes one-dimensional. We live in a world with no God in it. What happens on the human scene is all that is happening. Everything that needs to be done, we have to do. Whatever meaning, hope, or joy we wish to find, we must produce ourselves. The French existentialists insist on looking at life in that way. They strike me as very courageous, but to a man they come out feeling negative and hopeless. There really isn't any hope in the world or in our lives if we have no God in them.

Without being philosophers, we have all had experiences of life rising up and telling us it really isn't that way. When a person climbs to the peak of some mountain in the Rockies just at sunset and he or she sees the whole magnificent panorama of color and beauty spread out across the western sky, often the words come involuntarily, "O my God!" When a person runs out into the street to lift the crumpled body of a child just hit by a car, it would not be uncommon for those same words to burst forth: "O my God!"

In both cases there comes from somewhere deep within the awareness that something is going on in the world, something that touches the deepest and most precious meanings in our lives and over which we have no control. Both illustrations, one of joy and one of deep sorrow, are instinctive responses to the recognition of the awesomeness of a world we have not created. Life is not one dimensional.

Prayer is our response to God, our recognition that we don't live alone in this big, mysterious, sometimes frightening world. If who God is and what he feels are fuzzy to us, our responses will not be personal, but one way or another we can hardly help but respond. Even to resolve that we are going to live as if there is no God is a response, one that takes the power and importance of God with a high level of seriousness. You don't intentionally avoid a person who isn't important. Life just won't allow us to be authentically disinterested.

As a Christian pastor, I am convinced that in everything happening to us God is attempting to break through
and make contact. Relationship is what life is about, and
a personal response is what God wants from us. When the
contact is made, when we recognize who God is and who
we are in relation to him, life begins. Is prayer important?
It is a channel through which God pours himself and his
life into ours, allowing us to become fully-alive human
beings. In one of the finest and most scholarly books on
prayer ever written, Dr. George Buttrick said:

> Perhaps prayer in our time is the key-city of an irrepressible
> conflict. Perhaps our scientific agnosticism knows, though
> dimly, that if prayer can be riddled by argument or captured
> by scoffing the whole realm of religion will fall. Perhaps the
> badly shaken forces of religion also know, though dimly, that
> if prayer is renewed the prevalent skepticism must bow.[1]

Whatever God is, he can hardly be less than the finest
and best we know in our human relationships; and if the
fullness of our human relationships depends on deeply
personal and authentic communication, it would be hard
to exaggerate the pivotal place of prayer in our relationship with God. If prayer was necessary for Jesus to maintain the channel of power and meaning in his life, it can
hardly be unimportant to me.

Jesus' first disciples were fascinated by the meaning of
prayer in their Master's life. They had all grown up in a
religious community. Prayer should have been no inno-
vation to them; yet they came to Jesus and asked him to
teach them to pray. Many people are asking the same
question today. We shouldn't shame them or ourselves.
If talking in a creative and authentic way to other humans is difficult, what makes us think that talking to God
should be a snap?

Actually, just like our efforts to communicate with

---

1. George Buttrick, *Prayer* (New York: Abingdon Press,
1942), p. 16.

other human beings, our prayers reveal our feelings about God and ourselves. If we don't pray at all, we're saying God isn't important in our lives. We apparently think we can get along quite well on our own.

We must say also, however, that many people who seem to take God seriously and report that they pray all the time have some unusual notions about God and about themselves. Confronted with these notions, they would probably deny them, immediately and emphatically, but the character of their prayers tells on them. Prayer is not only response to God; the nature of our response indicates how we feel about the one to whom we're responding.

Some people, for example, feel committed and restricted to formal prayers. A man once told me that praying made him so nervous that he would probably faint if he were ever called upon to lead in prayer. There is a place for traditional prayers of the church, ones that have proven their usefulness to large numbers of people over a long period of time, but even these prayers must somehow become our own, or they are only the repetition of meaningless phrases. In many churches, including my own, it is common practice for the whole congregation to pray the Lord's Prayer together every Sunday. This is a meaningful part of the worship experience to me. It allows me to feel that I am getting the benefit of communicating with God in the words of one who was a master communicator. I feel the combined strength of the faith of other people who are praying with me. Praying the Lord's Prayer allows me to participate in the faith of Jesus Christ himself. That strengthens me as I am able to make his prayer my own.

On the other hand, if the only prayers we pray are formal and written, our picture of God and of ourselves is probably also formal and mechanical. We may have a correct picture of the majesty of God, but we miss the personal concern he reveals in Jesus Christ. If I am going to share with God from the unique and personal depths of my life, I must find some honest and personal terms in which to do it. I must dare to trust his love and caring.

Lots of prayers that I hear, and probably some that I pray, sound more like bargaining than praying. "If you'll get me out of this mess, I promise to be in church every Sunday for the rest of my life," or "If you'll help me get this new job, I promise to tithe every penny I make from it to the church." Do we think of God as one who makes deals? That's dangerous business.

A beautiful young mother once came to see me in great distress. Within the last two years she had been through major surgery twice. Her doctor had just told her she was going to have to go back into the hospital for another operation. That in itself was reason enough for great concern, but the rest of her story was almost more than I could bear.

Several years before, this woman's mother had a serious heart attack. At that time, the girl made a bargain with God. If he would allow her mother to live, she, the daughter, would permit him to do anything he wanted to her. Then these operations came on, one after another. She felt God was playing out his end of the bargain.

What kind of God is that? Hardly the one who has made himself and his purposes known to us in Jesus Christ! I wondered how this lovely young thing could possibly love such a capricious, unfeeling God. How could she live in a world whose God operates in that way? The bargaining approach to God distorts everything. It puts us in competition with God to see who can make the shrewdest deal. Life in this world becomes a contest with unfair odds.

Sometimes I run into devout people who really seem to think that their prayers can get God to change his mind. I know the story in the Old Testament about Abraham haggling with God to get him to save Sodom and Gomorrah, and I think there is some real meaning to it; but with the fuller disclosure of God's purposes in Christ, it has to read in a new light. What kind of regard do we show God when we operate on the assumption that he really doesn't know the best way to operate his world? What kind of image do we have of ourselves when we think we know better than God does just how things ought to go?

As I read the prayers of Jesus, I never find him demanding that God do this or that, not even for the sake of Jesus' own divine mission in the world. Those kinds of prayers have a "God Almightiness" to them that seems to me to have switched the proper roles. As a man said in a recent movie, "I know I'm God because I discovered that when I pray I'm talking to myself."

What I'm building to, if you hadn't already guessed or noticed, is "I Feel" prayers. That's the kind Jesus prayed. When he knelt in the Garden of Gethsemane, knowing his enemies would soon seize and kill him, his spirit was so troubled, says the Scripture, that he sweat great drops of blood. That's intense. Jesus was serious about the problem before him. He wasn't taking the threat and all that it seemed to say about the worth of his life with a casual nonchalance, but neither did he fall back into formal "good boy" prayers or whining prayers or bargaining prayers or demanding prayers. He let God know, exactly and authentically, what he was feeling, and he left God free to be God, to respond in any way he might choose.

Jesus didn't want to die, and he said so, not just once, but again and again. He wasn't trying to swing God around to his way of thinking. On the contrary, what Jesus wanted was to get his own will into line with God's. Jesus started where he was and said just how he felt. He was himself, in all his confusion and dread. It may bother us to think of Jesus as being confused, but he did say, "If it be thy will." Apparently he didn't know for sure. He followed his feeling, however, with another line, "Nevertheless, not my will but thine be done."

By being who he was, Jesus left the way open for God to be God. He made no demands as to what God had to do if he were really God. And God didn't desert him. Even in the awful, agonizing silence of the cross when Jesus *felt* utterly alone, God was at work shaping a miraculous Easter. Jesus trusted his real self to God, and God gave his real self and life to him. That, I think, is authentic and personal communication—real prayer.

In the early years of my ministry I got to know a most saintly soul. She is sensitive and deeply caring about others, intelligently and helpfully active in her church. One day her life fell apart. Her husband of twenty some years died—suddenly, unexpectedly, tragically. Not only did she lose a dearly loved companion around whose life her own had been organized, but for the first time since her marriage she was back out working for a living. Her whole life was suddenly filled with a constant succession of new and frightening experiences.

One day she told me what it felt like to come back to that empty house after work in the evening. She said that sometimes all she could do was scream. "Dammit-to-hell, God, I liked living with my husband better than I do with you!"

She said she knew even as she said it that a person isn't supposed to talk to God like that. But that's how she felt, so that's what she said, and a remarkable thing happened. Hardly would those bitter and painful words be out of her mouth before she began to get the feeling of strong and loving arms around her. It was almost as if she could hear God say, "I understand, my child. I understand."

I think her "I Feel" prayer was very Christian. I think it revealed her deep faith in God's personal concern for her and her confidence that God is big enough to take whatever her fears and feelings might be. Because she was able to be honest with God about how she felt, the barrier of pain and hurt that separated her from him (and from life, other people, and herself) was broken.

Her prayer put her back in touch with reality. She opened the channel which allowed God to come into her life.

From her long years in the church she knew that God had already addressed her; she had heard often about Jesus calling the "weary and heavy laden" to come to him. So she came, just as she was; and she found that it was not an empty invitation. God called and she responded. That's what prayer is—taking God's Word to us seriously and personally, and responding out of our authentic depths. That woman taught me more about prayer than anyone else I have ever known.

Prayer isn't a means of conning God into doing what we want or fulfilling a religious obligation so that God will be good to us or telling God how he ought to run his world. Prayer is a means of entering into a personal relationship, being who we really are and allowing God to be who he really is. Whenever that happens, whether it be between two humans or between some person and God, a miracle occurs—the miracle of new life. Those kinds of relationships are what this life God gives us is all about, and authentic relationships are the only ones worth having.

11

GOD'S ALMIGHTY STATEMENT

Only one person is qualified to make "God Almighty" statements, but he doesn't. God's most decisive, revealing statement to us is in an "I Feel" form. "In the beginning was the Word, and the Word was with God, and the Word was God. He was in the beginning with God; all things were made through him, and without him was not anything made that was made. In him was life, and the life was the light of men. The light shines in the darkness, and the darkness has not overcome it. . . . And the Word became flesh and dwelt among us, full of grace and truth; we have beheld his glory, glory as of the only Son from the Father" (John 1:1–5, 14).

Jesus Christ is the Word. He is God's Almighty Statement to us. The Word God sends to us is a feeling Word, a personal Word, a human Word. In the Word God lets us know who he is, what he wants, and how he feels, leaving himself vulnerable to ridicule and rejection. When the Word he sends is not received, God suffers, but he does not become defensive or apologetic, nor does he withdraw himself or his love from us. Jesus Christ is the Word above all words, behind all words, and on which all authentic words are built. He is the Truth, the personal embodiment of all that is and is to be, the only completely authentic Word.

God could have spoken to us in some other way. We fail to appreciate the deep significance of the manner in which God does speak unless we realize that he had other options. Understanding this, we are more likely to give serious attention to how God speaks.

Many Christians unduly emphasize the words of Scripture, as if they were the fullest expression of God's communication to us. If God had wanted to communicate through written words, he certainly could have done so without subjecting his Son to the pain and humiliation of life among jealous, fearful people and the agony of dying on a cross. If written words were to be the basis for our knowledge of God, life, and ourselves, then God could surely have written those words in a way that would be less confusing and less susceptible to misinterpretations and awkward translations.

The constant insistence of the Christian community is that God has not made his fullest revelation to us in words, but in the Word—in Jesus Christ, a living, acting, feeling person—and all the words of Scripture bear witness to the Word. Those words are essential for us who do not have the opportunity to know the Word in the flesh, but those words never become the same as the Word. The words derive their truth, meaning, and living vitality from him who is the living Word and who can never be enclosed in any set of words, rules, doctrines, or propositions.

If we allow the words of Scripture to become the objects of our faith, we can be said to be taking God literally but not seriously. That needs to be reversed. God is not satisfied to be known in the words we read. He has gone to a great deal of trouble to let us know him in a personal way. To take God seriously is to deal seriously with what God has done.

To take the words of Scripture literally is to assume that God has somehow enclosed himself in words of Hebrew and Greek (none of which are available to us in their original manuscript form), the full meaning of which does not suffer from translation across many centuries, from an ancient agrarian society to a modern industrial society. But even more important than these linguistic problems is the fundamental question of how we believe God makes himself and his purposes known— through words or the Word.

To take God seriously, I believe, is to recognize that what he has to communicate to us is so much more than words. I myself have known the utter frustration of attempting to communicate something of deep importance to me to other people, something so meaningful and deep that no words could fully express it. But the people insisted on taking me literally, which was the same as refusing to understand me. Surely this must be something like how God feels when he sees people getting all hung-up and arguing back and forth about the words of Scripture. Surely something within him cries out, "Look at what I've done! Look at what I mean! Look at what I feel! Look at what I want to give you! Look at the Word!" God wants to be taken seriously.

No one's words can really be understood apart from a knowledge of the person who speaks them and how they are spoken. We must look through the words of Scripture to see the Word who stands behind them. If we are to understand those words, we must get a feel for the purposes and passions of the person to whom they bear witness. What does he want? What does his life mean? What is God saying to me in his Word?

Of this much we can be sure: What God has to communicate to us can only be fully expressed in a living, feeling, personal, human life. That's the way God himself has chosen to speak to us.

God speaks to us as he does because of who he is. He is not cold, mechanical logic. He is not distant, detached wisdom. He is not a fickle potentate who rewards those who honor him properly and destroys those who fail to please him. God, as he makes himself known in Jesus Christ, is almighty wisdom and power and all the other exalted attributes we can imagine, but all of these are contained within and are consistent with his being personal. God is love. God cares, weeps, rejoices, yearns, suffers. God feels as well as thinks.

So God communicates with us as he does because any other way would be less than expressive of his authentic nature. To think of God or his truth as disembodied rules or propositions is to misunderstand what God reveals about himself in the Word.

Second, God speaks to us as he does because of who we are. The unique thing about human beings, that is, what makes them distinct from the rest of creation, is our capacity to respond to God and to each other, to live in deeply personal relationships of love.

To live in that kind of relationship, however, is always a choice. We have to choose to be human. A tree doesn't choose to be a tree, and a dog doesn't choose to be a dog, but we are not truly human unless we choose to be. And we can choose not to be human. We are aware of that when we speak of "inhuman treatment."

To choose to be human is to choose to live in relationships of love, with God and with other people, and it's always a choice. Otherwise it's not a personal relationship. If I love someone because I have to or because I'm afraid not to, that isn't love, and what I have with that person is not a loving relationship. Whatever attention or affection I show him or her will be a coerced expression of my fear, not a personally chosen response of my love.

So God, who deliberately created us to be human, persons created in his image and with the capacity for reflecting his personal nature in our lives, respects the choice he has given us. He does not overwhelm our senses with some spectacular display of his power or terrify our imaginations with colossal threats or manipulate our thinking with irrefutable logic. He respects and protects our right and responsibility to choose.

God knows not only how we are because he created us, but how we arc because of our sin—our state of being which leaves us separated from him, from one another, and from ourselves. How does one deal with a separated, alienated person? Not by coercion or force; that would only increase the alienation. If there is a sincere desire to make contact with an alienated person, the one desiring the contact must be willing to come to the separated one where he or she is—willing to suffer rebuff and rejection, willing to share the pain of loneliness and isolation, willing to understand the fear that separation breeds. This is how the Word comes to us in the world. God speaks to us as he does because of who we are, how we are, and what he wills us to be.

Which brings us to the third reason God speaks to us as he does—because of what he wants. The phrase "the will of God" is tossed around in so many different ways and with so many different meanings that it is little wonder most people are confused, eventually beginning to wonder if there *is* a will of God or even a God! To the best of my understanding, Dr. Reuel Howe has it right when he says, "The only will of God that anyone can be certain about is that God wills for us to be and to be in relation." [1]

God wills for us to be, to be responsible, choice-making persons, to be whole human beings. This is the consistent biblical testimony as to what God is about in the world. In Old Testament and New, God is at work in the world

---

1. Reuel Howe, *Survival Plus* (New York: Seabury Press, 1971), p. 114.

freeing people from whatever holds and binds them, setting them free in order that they may be. As we study his teachings and his life, we begin to see that nothing is more important to Jesus Christ than the worth and integrity of every individual human life. For our right to be, he lived and died and rose again. An expression of loving concern shown for another human being, no matter how lowly, Jesus identifies as an expression of love for him and as a validation that we have understood and participated in the meaning of life. God wills for us to be.

And God wills for us to be in relation. The whole direction of creation is toward union, bringing back together that which has been separated. Christ came to bring us back into relationship with God, and he has commissioned us to be the ambassadors of his reconciling love to others.

So God speaks to us in such a way that we are free to be, and he opens to us the door to relationship. By speaking in a different way—with a show of force or through a rigid set of rules or by means of a wisdom to be learned and memorized—God could have gotten order and obedience, but not what he wants: whole persons able to live and love in relationship.

But doesn't God lose his honor and authority by speaking in this way? We are concerned about honor and authority (because deep down we fear we don't have any), but God isn't (because he does). God isn't worried about maintaining his image. He knows he is God, so he has nothing to prove. Having nothing to prove, he is able to be who he is.

Some of Jesus' disciples were offended when their Master and his message were not received. They wanted Jesus to call down fire from heaven to destroy those impertinent nogoodniks, but Jesus refused. He had not come to prove his strength. He had come to let people know of God's love and forgiveness and acceptance. He was the Word, so he didn't have to prove it. As Paul wrote to the people of Philippi, Jesus emptied himself of the glory of

being God in order to serve God's purposes and God's
people—allowing people to be and to be in relation—and
that fulfilling of God's loving purposes was his glory.

Jesus was able to speak and to act appropriately in
every situation because he was free from any necessity
to prove or impress. He was speaking and acting from his
integrity. He, who had come from God, knew who God is
and was able to say so, not with proofs and fine arguments. He steadfastly refused to use miracles to prove
himself or his cause. He spoke from the integrity of who
he was, which preserved the integrity of those to whom
he spoke. He protected their freedom to make a personal
response.

He, through whom all things had been created, knew
what life is all about, so he told us, not by arguments or
threats, but on the basis of who he was in himself. In a
memorable encounter with the "woman by the well"
(John 4), Jesus saw through to the depths of the woman's
life. He wasn't thrown off by the deceptive disguises she
wore to protect the pain and shame of her life. He spoke
to her in a straightforward manner, with authority, but
he didn't shame or mock her. He didn't try to correct her
at her expense. Perhaps the most notable aspect of the
dialogue is that the woman, though stripped of her de-
fenses and corrected in her misunderstandings, still felt
understood and accepted. And acceptance is not something she was likely to have expected, not from her
neighbors, let alone from a man of religion. Here was a
man who knew her through and through, who told her
everything she had ever done; and yet he accepted her!
Though he spoke with authority, Jesus had nothing to
prove—only a life to share—and that's how he came across.

Jesus was able to speak with authority without being
authoritarian. He had no ulterior motive. Because he is
the Way, he knows where we will find our lives. So he
said to his disciples, "He who finds his life will lose it,

but he who loses his life for my sake will find it" (Matt. 10:39).

I mentioned earlier the importance of reading the words of Scripture in light of the Word. This is a case in point. Jesus wasn't threatening his disciples; he was instructing them. He was sending them out to bear witness to what they knew, and he did the same for them. He told them what he knew. Later, speaking to some of those same disciples, Jesus asked them to stay and watch with him through the long and agonizing night before his crucifixion. He wanted their friendship and their closeness, so he asked for it, but he didn't get it. He demanded nothing; he asked for what he wanted. In both these situations Jesus spoke to the disciples from his integrity. He was willing to be who he was, to feel what he felt, to say what was authentically within him, without fear for his image.

Obviously Jesus did not put an "I Feel" before every statement he uttered (and neither do I suggest that we do so), but he did speak within the guidelines for an "I Feel" statement. Without any effort to intimidate, manipulate, or impress, he spoke and acted authentically from his integrity. He spoke in order to communicate— to know and to be known. He who is the Word, God's feeling and personal communication of himself to us, spoke personal and feeling words.

All this is a reflection of God's wholeness. Jesus said, "You, therefore, must be perfect, as your heavenly Father is perfect" (Matt. 5:48). That verse has caused a lot of trouble. What we associate with the word *perfect* is not what is meant in this passage, and many people, struggling to live up to their understanding of *perfect,* have become terribly anxious and artificial and frighteningly judgmental of others.

The Greek word is *teleois,* and "wholeness" is a much more accurate and understandable translation of it for our day. The instruction is that we are to be whole in the same way that God is whole, and lest there be any confusion about what that means, the paragraph of which this verse is the last sentence tells us clearly. The wholeness of God is that "he makes his sun rise on the evil and on the good, and sends rain on the just and on the unjust" (Matt. 5:45).

God is whole in that he acts out of his integrity in a way consistent with his purposes, no matter what we do or don't do in response. Even when we deny and defy him, God's character and purposes do not change. He is whole.

William Barclay's commentary on this passage helps to clarify it further.

> So then a man will be *teleois* if he fulfills the purpose for which he was created. For what purpose was man created? The Bible leaves us in no doubt as to that. "Let us make man in our own image and after our likeness." Man was created to be like God. The characteristic of God is this universal benevolence, this unconquerable good will, this constant seeking of the highest good for every man. The great characteristic of God is to love saint and sinner alike. No matter what men do to him, God seeks nothing but their highest good.[2]

The wholeness of God lies in his purpose to act rather than react, and he acts according to the integrity of who he is. *This is the wholeness which Jesus Christ commands of us!* We are to be who we are, persons created in God's image, capable of living in relationships of love and speaking and acting with the same authenticity we see in the Word.

As Barclay says, "We are to be like God," but this doesn't mean we are to pretend that we *are* God. We are to be like God in our wholeness, in our integrity, and in our ability to love even those who do not love us, but the minute we begin thinking, acting, and speaking as if we are God, we lose our integrity. Of course, we know we

---

2. William Barclay, *The Gospel of Matthew,* vol. 1 (Philadelphia: Westminster Press, 1958), p. 114.

are not God, but we often speak as if we possessed all wisdom and knowledge. "This is how it is!" To speak in this way is to surrender our humanity and our wholeness. We are human beings, loved by God and called to be instruments of his love to others. When we are that, we are whole.

Our wholeness grows out of our communicative relationship with God and other people. Jesus Christ not only commands us to be whole as God is whole, but he makes it possible for us to be so. That is the Word we must hear behind the words. If it were not so, Jesus' command to us would be bad news indeed!

What keeps us from being whole? Our fear. We fear that if people knew us as we really are, they wouldn't like or respect us. We know we have a great difficulty liking and respecting ourselves. There are all those dark, dirty things we have done. What if people found out? Horrors! Besides all that, there is that even greater load of wicked things we have thought. Who would be our friend if all that were revealed?

So we play a role or, more likely, many roles, but inside we're something else. What hope is there for us ever to be whole persons?

Jesus Christ is our hope. He who knows us better than we know ourselves has looked at all that we are, and he says he is *for* us. Even more than that, he has *shown* that he is *for* us. Even the grim reality of death was not enough to cause him to give up on us. The fact that God is *for* us is a historical reality.

You know how good it makes you feel when some friend, someone to whom you have revealed a part of your hidden self, says, "I think you're OK"? The day becomes perceptibly brighter. You find a new strength and confidence welling up within you. You feel a capability for coping with life and its problems you didn't have before—all because somebody knows you and likes you and believes in you, somebody flesh-and-blood real, not a philosophical or psychological proposition but a feeling person.

With that picture in mind, think what it would be like if God, the Creator of all that is, were to say to you, with a flesh-and-blood reality, "I love you. I accept you. You are precious and worthwhile and useful just as you are."

Well, that is exactly what God has said and is saying to you in the Word, in Jesus Christ. He is God's Almighty Statement. This is much more than being understood and accepted by a friend. This is the giant affirmation from the highest, deepest, and fullest. This is what God is communicating to us in the Word. There is no condemnation for those who are in Christ Jesus. In a flesh-and-blood reality God lets us know how he feels about us. God is *for* us.

But how do we hear that Word, appropriate it, and become whole? Let me put it another way. How do we become a part of any communicative relationship? We listen to what is being said beneath and through the words to catch the deep meaning. We receive it and respond to it.

God says he is *for* us, and Jesus Christ is the living reality of that affirmation. Jesus Christ asks us to believe in him. He does not call for faith in a set of propositions but in himself. To receive and respond to the Word is to believe him. An appropriate response to what God is saying to us might go like this: "I believe that you are *for* me. Jesus says I am of worth, and I believe him in spite of what others may say about me and even what I may say about myself. I believe I am who Christ says I am. I hear the Word. I accept him and believe him."

By entering a communicative relationship with God we begin the process of becoming whole—no longer divided and at war within ourselves, no longer hiding and role playing and deceiving. We find the joy of a new life in being who we really are rather than trying to act out what we think others expect of us. The Word—heard, received, believed, and responded to—becomes the basis for a whole life.

Hans Hofmann describes this new basis for whole and mature living.

> It is the loving acceptance of God which, exactly because of its unconditional nature, jealously forbids this person to base his sense of justification, acceptability, or worth on anything else but this divine basis for his existence. The critical element in the judgment of God enters at the point when a person asks himself whether he is so confident of God's acceptance that he no longer depends on any image of himself, and therefore can face freely and honestly the positive as well as the negative aspects of his personality. The God-given freedom to face oneself provides the stimulus for confident treatment of those aspects of one's own personality which indeed allow improvement. It also provides the reassuring experience that from difficulty can grow a more mature and dependable personality structure.[3]

The wholeness we begin to experience as we enter a trusting, communicative relationship with the Word finds its growth in our communicative relationships with others. Jesus said his disciples can make it in the world without faking a wisdom or power or authority or goodness they do not have. As a reflection of their faith in the Word, their words can be trusted because they have spoken them. The Word sets them free to be. There is no conflict between what they are and what they say.

Jesus specified all this in a passage found in Matthew 5:33–37. Here Jesus forbids his disciples to swear by any being, place, or authority outside themselves. They don't need it. Those who, finding themselves in a tight spot or losing an argument, throw in the name of some nationally known expert or run to the encyclopedia or the Bible to reinforce their faltering case, show themselves to be fearful and unwhole people. It's like when a person says,

3. Hans Hofmann, *Religion and Mental Health* (New York: Harper & Bros., 1961), p. 249.

"By God, I really mean it!" He or she is confessing that he or she wouldn't expect to be believed if speaking only on personal authority. But by using the name of God he or she is hoping to be taken seriously. Such a person reveals a lack of faith in his or her selfhood and integrity. No matter how loudly he or she may shout, such a person is deeply unsure of himself or herself.

We all know what happens when something like that gets started in a conversation. You pull in some outside authority to give weight to your argument, and the other person reaches for another authority to do battle with yours. It's like two little boys who assail each other with the hypothetical boast that "My dad can beat up your dad!" Nothing gets settled. The dads don't fight. Lots of words get thrown around and feelings get hurt, but nothing gets settled. Whoever wins and whoever loses, no real growth or communication happens. The boys go away as they came, fearful and alone—only more so. Such non-communication destroys wholeness.

Jesus, who opens up the possibility of wholeness for us by initiating a relationship of communication between us and God, directs us to grow in wholeness through communicative relationships with others. In the passage I just mentioned, the one in which Jesus forbade the use of outside authorities to strengthen our words, Jesus went on to instruct his disciples to say simply yes and no, in other words, to say what they mean, to speak from their integrity. Because they know themselves to be worthwhile and important persons, they need no deceptive, defensive, or destructive rhetoric, just a simple declaration of "This is how it is with me. This is how I see it."

When we talk like that, we open up a whole new world to the persons with whom we speak. When it begins to dawn on them that we aren't going to attack them with outside authorities or belittle them with purported wisdom, they don't have to defend themselves. If we will meet them and deal with them as the persons we are—

full of both strengths and weaknesses, faith and doubt, courage and fear, love and hate—they can dare to be who they are in relation to us. A miraculous thing happens when two people meet authentically: life. We find strength, hope, courage, acceptance, and love flowing through the relationship and into us.

The Apostle Paul told us that if anyone is in Christ he is a new creation; surely this is a significant part of what it means to be in Christ. When we allow his acceptance to free us from the need to defend or deceive, daring by his grace to be who we really are, then other people can know and trust us. As they experience our acceptance, they can relax their fearful compulsions to impress and intimidate. They can begin to experiment with being who they are without pretensions. Enclosed within the acceptance and love of God in Jesus Christ, both of us become more whole and more alive than we've ever been before—new creations!

Parents no longer have to maintain their authority image in front of their kids, and kids no longer have to prove to their parents that they don't care. Husbands can let their wives know when they're frightened, and wives don't have to play games to let their husbands know they want to be appreciated. Church members don't have to live up to a stereotype of righteousness to feel worthwhile, and nonchurch people are denied the excuse of staying away because they don't want to be hypocrites. The Word is that it's OK for us to be who we are, and starting from there we grow.

When the Word God sends is received and responded to, we find the courage to be, and through the communication of our authentic words, others are able to hear the Word also and live. The process is so fantastic that Paul could hardly believe what was happening. "Why, it's as if God is making his appeal to you through us!" (paraphrase of 2 Cor. 5:20).

The church is that fellowship of people who have heard

and received the Word and who share it through their lives with others. The problem is that all too often the church gets scared and panicky just as individuals do. The church sometimes begins to worry that the world isn't going to respect them or take them seriously or that even people within the fellowship will not respond or behave as they should. When this happens, the church begins to shut its ears to the Word and begins putting a lot of stress on words—making rules, publishing pronouncements, and haggling over doctrine as if there were something magic in the phraseology.

But it doesn't work. All the fearful things which got the church into this uptight position in the first place become even more evident. People experience the church as mechanical, rigid, and judgmental. That's not what they need. They already feel guilty and frightened enough without the church loading on more guilt and fear. So they walk away from the church or continue to ignore it if they weren't there in the first place.

Those people may think they're rejecting God, but in actuality they're rejecting some "God Almighty" statements made by frightened men and women.

The church is reborn when some people find themselves listening to the Word instead of fussing and fuming about words. When they hear the Word and believe it, their lives begin to change, and so do the words they speak. They become different in the way they feel about themselves and in the way they talk and relate to other people. Instead of judgment and condemnation they speak words of understanding and compassion. Instead of struggling so hard to make people religious they work for justice and peace for all people. They throw their energies into the creation of a society in which all people have opportunity to be and to be in relation.

The Word gets around. People notice the difference in those people over at the church, a good kind of difference. They see people who listen and care, people who aren't all fired up to divide the world into those who are going to hell and those who aren't. They see something both warm and tough, something both human and divine. That's exciting and appealing. The people who see it and experience it want to know more about it; they want to hear, feel, and share whatever is going on in the church.

God's Almighty Statement to us, the Word of his truth and love and acceptance in Jesus Christ, is our hope for life and wholeness. The Word does not come dogmatically but humanly, authentically, and respectfully, asking to be received and believed. When the Word *is* received, believed, and shared, there are new persons and a new world.

> How silently, how silently
> The wondrous gift is given!
> So God imparts to human hearts
> The blessing of his heaven.
> No ear may hear his coming,
> But in this world of sin,
> Where meek souls will receive Him, still
> The dear Christ enters in.[4]

4. Phillips Brooks, "O Little Town of Bethlehem."

12

I GIVE YOU PERMISSION

The "God Almighty" statements/"I Feel" statements concept is a tool for opening up channels of communication with God, other people, and ourselves, but it is also much more. If it is employed as a gimmick, it is misused, and it is just as susceptible to legalism and game playing as any other device. The crucial element is attitude.

When a person understands the basis in Scripture and the reality in human experience on which this approach is built, the "God Almighty" statements/"I Feel" statements device begins to lead him or her into a new awareness of who he or she really is in the world and of who other people are. If a person, a couple, or a family agrees to enter into a contract to communicate in "I Feel" statements and does so with a sincere desire to make contact with themselves and one another, they can expect exciting results.

This new awareness of oneself is the important experience; it is growth. An "I Feel" person begins to receive life and its experiences in a new way. He or she even begins to think differently and be a more relaxed, thankful, joyful person. Instead of thinking of oneself as a poor, forsaken orphan in the world, one who must scratch, bite, and claw to get anywhere near a fair share of what is to be had, one begins to see oneself as a person to whom much has been given—everything necessary for a whole, authentic human life. Instead of demanding of life and God and other people (and feeling one never gets as much as one deserves), the "I Feel" person finds inexpressible joy going about in the world, sharing his or her hope and life, giving others permission "to be."

A group of people had been meeting together for weeks in therapy sessions. They had come to know one another pretty well. They knew what to expect. Sue could be counted on to be dramatic and make a big, emotional scene out of every little nothing. Dan would never say much and usually took refuge in a shell of silence. Paul was a clown, the guy who made a big joke out of everything. They had one another pretty well figured out, but sometimes they realized they didn't really know one another at all. They still went home wondering "What is he really like?" "What does she really think?"

So they said, "This is no good!" We're supposed to be getting to know one another and ourselves. We never will this way. Let's quit playing games. We've got to start being who we really are. Sue, get off the big actress routine. We have no Oscars to give. Quit using us as your audience. Just level with us. Let us know how you really feel. Come on, Dan, climb out of your shell. Open up. We're not going to bite you. Let us in on those deep waters that run so silently beneath the surface. Knock it off, Paul. We've had enough of your jokes. We know your life isn't one big circus. Tell us what you're really feeling inside."

So Sue and Dan and Paul all tried. They didn't want to be phonies. They wanted to be real. That's why they were there. But they couldn't seem to do it. They wanted to get their feelings out, but they just couldn't.

Being dramatic was all Sue knew how to do. She'd been doing it all her life. To throw all that away would be like taking your clothes off in the middle of Grand Central Station. Dan wanted to talk, but he felt sure that if he did it would be apparent he was a dummy. Everyone would laugh at him. Paul was afraid that if people ever quit laughing at him they might not notice him at all. He didn't like being a clown all the time, but it was a whole lot safer than letting people know how scared and weak he felt inside. They all tried, but they couldn't do it.

The therapist in the group knew how hard they were trying, but he also knew that changes would never happen that way. So he went around the room, speaking to each one, letting him or her know how he felt. Instead of demanding feelings from them, he gave them his.

"Sue, I give you permission to be an actress. I understand your fear that if you don't play Sarah Bernhardt all the time you might not get any attention at all.

"Dan, I give you permission to be silent. I understand how much you want to break open but can't. I give you permission just to sit there.

"Paul, I give you permission to be a clown. I understand that you don't always feel happy and cheerful, but you can tell us about it when you feel ready."

A very remarkable thing began to happen. The tensions began to fade. Each person felt a certain warm glow. "I *am* understood! It's OK for me to be who I am. There's no "God Almighty" demand or judgment being laid on me. I don't have to achieve some impossible task in order to be accepted." It was relaxing and also exciting.

Sue had been given permission to be an actress. She didn't have to be defensive or self-conscious about her manner any more, and that freedom allowed her to think about it and talk about it. She found herself telling the group how phony and uncomfortable she felt sometimes doing her big scene, but she didn't know how to get out of it. She said, "I feel that people expect me to perform, and if I don't, I feel they will be disappointed in me." As she told her story, she began to laugh and then to cry, but this time not for dramatic effect. It was all real, and the group understood. Because they knew how Sue felt, they had a sense of knowing her. It felt very, very good to be able to share Sue's feelings.

Dan had been given permission to be silent. He no longer had to feel guilty or awkward. Strangely enough, he soon found that he wanted to talk, and he talked as he never had before. He talked about how fearful he was of appearing stupid and how angry he got sometimes when everyone else was talking and having a good time. "I feel lots of times that the rest of you don't even care that I exist!" Dan's heart was really pounding! He was talking, and no one was snickering or turning away. It felt good. Dan didn't feel so trapped or closed in any more. His feelings were coming out; and as they came out, so did Dan.

Paul had been given permission to be a clown. Before he knew it, he heard himself saying, "I suppose you think I enjoy trying to be a funny man all the time. Well, let me tell you, I don't! Sometimes I feel like crying. Sometimes I want to be taken seriously but someone always says, 'Well, look at old Paul! My, what a weighty philosopher our old comedian has become!'" But as Paul looked around, he discovered that the group *was* taking him seriously. They were hearing *him!* There was no ridicule or pity, just understanding. He was telling them how he felt, and they accepted him. It was very, very good. Change follows acceptance, not the other way around.

As Jesus came riding into Jericho one day he spotted a squirrelly little man up in a tree. The man hated himself. Did Jesus know? The man was despised by his neighbors. He was a quisling. He had sold out to the hated Romans. He was getting rich by collecting exorbitant taxes from his own countrymen. Did Jesus know?

Zacchaeus didn't like being that kind of man. Sometimes he felt he would gladly trade his fastback chariot and his fifty-yard-line seats at the coliseum just to be "one of the guys." But the people wouldn't let him. He was a traitor. That's what they expected him to be, and that's what he was. There was no way he could change. His yearnings for a different life lay buried beneath years of rejection and disappointment. It was almost as if God himself had decreed it. Zacchaeus was a nogoodnik!

Jesus must have sensed what was going on in Zacchaeus. As he rode by the tree where the little traitor was perched, Jesus let Zacchaeus know what he was feeling. He risked Zacchaeus' rejection and scorn from the crowd. He made an "I Feel" statement: "Zacchaeus, I want to be with you today."

Jesus didn't say he would like Zacchaeus after he had changed or made amends for all his cheating. He said, "I want to be with you today." Zacchaeus could hardly believe his ears. "Just as I am? This despised and worthless me? Can it be that I matter to him, to this holy man? Is it possible that he sees something worthwhile in me?"

"So he made haste and came down, and received him joyfully. And when they saw it they all murmured, 'He has gone in to be the guest of a man who is a sinner.' And Zacchaeus stood and said to the Lord, 'Behold, Lord, the half of my goods I give to the poor; and if I have defrauded any one of anything, I restore it fourfold.' And Jesus said to him, 'Today salvation has come to this house, since he also is a son of Abraham. For the Son of man came to seek and to save the lost'" (Luke 19:6–10).

Talk about change! But it did not come about as a result of any "God Almighty" demand. Jesus knew the yearning for life and respect that had Zacchaeus up a tree and out on a limb. Jesus accepted him as he was; he gave Zacchaeus permission to be who he was even though to do so meant accepting a lot of things *in him* which contradicted Jesus' whole ministry.

A small thing, perhaps, accepting Zacchaeus, but it cost

Jesus the friendship of the good and proper people of Jericho. They were furious! A small thing, perhaps, giving persons permission to be who they are, but it was no small thing to Zacchaeus. It was the biggest thing that had ever happened to him. He had a new understanding of how God felt about him. Jesus' acceptance gave Zacchaeus the freedom to turn his life a full 180 degrees. Change follows acceptance, not the other way around.

Zacchaeus no longer had to fight for status or prove that he was a person of worth or cry himself to sleep at night for the respect his riches could not buy. Now he knew, because he believed Jesus, how God felt about him, and the message had come through a personal relationship of acceptance and respect. The Scriptures say he received Jesus "joyfully." Zacchaeus had been given what he could not purchase at any price. Jesus gave him permission to be. Zacchaeus received it and believed it and became. ("The only will of God that anyone can be certain about is that he wills for us to be and to be in relation.")

Jesus walks through the Gospels letting people know how he feels about them, giving them God's permission to come alive—a woman caught in the act of adultery, a man whose mind was deranged by a thousand tormenting thoughts, a boy who dared to suggest that his sack lunch might feed five thousand men. Jesus accepted them as they were for what they were, treated them with respect, told them they were useful. He didn't judge them. He gave them permission to be. Some accepted his gift and some did not, but all who accepted his gift came alive with the wholeness of joy.

Jesus walks through the world today doing the same thing. He lets us know how God *feels* about us. He gives us God's friendship, understanding, and acceptance. He gives us God's permission to come alive, but he makes no "God Almighty" demands as to how we must change in order to receive him.

Are you losing confidence in yourself as a parent? Jesus

Christ gives you permission to be the parent you are. He understands your torment. He knows how desperately you want to be a good parent. Who you are is enough. Just be it.

Are you losing hope in your marriage? Jesus Christ gives you permission to be discouraged. He understands how much you yearn for love, how desperately you ache for some indication that you are prized and appreciated. He gives you that love and appreciation. They are yours. That's how God feels about you. You can believe it.

Do you feel like a phony? Jesus Christ understands. Are you afraid? Jesus Christ understands. Do you drink too much? Jesus Christ understands what a torment that is. You don't have to make up a lot of defensive rationalizations. Jesus Christ says that all God feels for you is compassion and affection. He gives you permission to be who you are.

As long as we concentrate all our attention on correcting a problem, the problem has all our attention. Jesus directs our attention to how God feels about us, to God's confidence in us. That's what we really need more than anything else.

Maybe this sounds crazy to you. You think, "Give a guy permission to be who he is and he'll go dead on the vine, think he's got it made, quit trying." At least I know I have a devil of a time getting that thought out of my mind, but Jesus says it doesn't work that way. Jesus says that only when you give a person permission to be who he or she is does he or she have the real possibility of becoming a child of God, a whole human being.

Think about it for a minute. The only time we ever make a real confession of our wrong, the kind that represents a sincere desire to change, is when we know we are already forgiven before we confess. If a husband thought his wife would throw him out if he told her the truth, he never would tell her. It's the knowledge that we are already loved, accepted, and forgiven that allows us to examine our lives and change them. God lets us know how he feels about us. He gives us the freedom of his love as an opportunity to live, and he gives it before we have done anything to merit or earn it. He gives it now. He says, "This is how I feel about you. I love you—now!"

Jesus accepted Zacchaeus as he was; and within the power of that magnificent love, Zacchaeus became more of a man than he had ever dreamed possible. Because he received and believed the acceptance Jesus gave him, Zacchaeus was able to accept himself. He was on the road to wholeness.

There's only one other thing I can think of to match the thrill of being accepted. That is to spend your life accepting other people, giving them permission to be who they are. Then we become co-workers with God in what he's doing in the world. Talk about a meaningful life!

The minute we quit trying to bend other people around to make them what we want them to be, a tremendous weight rolls off our shoulders—the weight of trying to be God Almighty. What's more, if we mean it and stick with it, that other person's hostility might begin to recede. When a person doesn't have to fortify himself or herself to deal with you as God any more, his or her defensive energies are transformed into dealing with you as a person. He or she becomes more fully human, and so do you.

Giving other people permission to be who they are is costly. It was for Jesus, and it is for us. But it is the way God has chosen to bring his kingdom on earth.

It all begins with our willingness to receive God's Almighty Statement, our willingness to believe that we matter to God, personally and eternally. When we believe that, we experience new freedom, joy, and release in our lives. We find we are strong, confident, and able to be.

God's acceptance becomes real for us when we make it the basis for accepting ourselves. Then we no longer feel we have to measure up to some ideal in order to prove that we matter. We live in a posture of humble confidence

—humble because we know we are not God, confident because we know we are the recipients of his full, personal, and unending love. We can live, just as we are, and nothing can destroy us!

Life becomes dynamic when we use our lives to give other people permission to be, sharing with them God's Almighty "I Feel" Statement. When people experience from us that they do not have to conform to our "God Almighty" demands, they learn to enjoy being who they are. They discover that they really do matter and life begins.

That's the power for changing life that modern psychology has discovered, but psychology didn't invent it. It's been changing lives for a long time. It's the power of God in Jesus Christ. He is God's authentic Word to us.